"When we think of people who best model what missions ought to be, Herb and Jessie Nehlsen are at the top of the list. Nothing better can be said than that they gave their lives lovingly.

—Dr. David Rambo

"Myra Brown has masterfully captured the life journey and gracious hearts of two people who have given their utmost for the cause of Christ in the world. . . . This is truly a story of great faith, great vision, great compassion and great heart."

—Terry Young, Senior Pastor
First Alliance Church, Calgary, Canada

"This amazing and sometimes amusing story is a reminder that God chooses the most unlikely candidates to do His work, perhaps because they know they can't do it on their own, and because they never doubt Who gets the credit."

—Phil Callaway, Author
Editor of *Servant* magazine

"An insightful account of God's faithfulness that should be passed on to the next generation."

—Dr. Miriam Charter
Canadian Theological Seminary

"A gripping biography of an extraordinary missionary couple. . . . Though Herb and Jessie are a hard act to follow, the reader is left with the strong conviction that there are unlimited opportunities open to anyone totally committed to God. Well worth reading!"

—Dr. Raymur Downey, Vice President
C&MA Global Ministries

"Uncle Herb and Aunt Jessie are two of my best loved people. . . . As an MK, being on the receiving end of huge hugs and great love, and then as a missionary colleague, working with them side by side, my life has never ceased to be challenged by the passion they have for the lost."

—Nansie Ike, missionary
Abidjan, Côte d'Ivoire

"This story reminds us that God calls ordinary people and uses their unique gifts, personalities and abilities to build His kingdom."

—Joanne Beach, President
Alliance Women Canada

"Meeting Herb meant obtaining a life-long memory. I have been inspired by the exemplary life he and Jessie led."

—Dr. Ruth Rambo

"With the clarity and sensitivity of a practitioner, Myra Brown introduces another missionary couple to the Jaffray Series."

—Dr. Garth Leno, Regional Director
Samaritan's Purse

"Herb and Jessie didn't *play* a servant role, they *were* servants. Such words as humor, helping hands and hunger for holiness describe them. This book shows what God can do through people who are dedicated to Him and to the people they serve."

—Rev. Arie Verduijn, Director
CAMA Zending, CMA Holland

Larger than Life

Larger than Life

The Story of
Herbert and Jessie Nehlsen

Myra Brown

✠ CHRISTIAN PUBLICATIONS, INC.
CAMP HILL, PENNSYLVANIA

✚CHRISTIAN PUBLICATIONS, INC.
3825 Hartzdale Drive, Camp Hill, PA 17011
www.christianpublications.com

Faithful, biblical publishing since 1883

Larger than Life:
The Story of Herbert and Jessie Nehlsen
ISBN: 0-87509-959-9
© 2002 by Myra Brown
All rights reserved
Printed in the United States of America

02 03 04 05 06   5 4 3 2 1

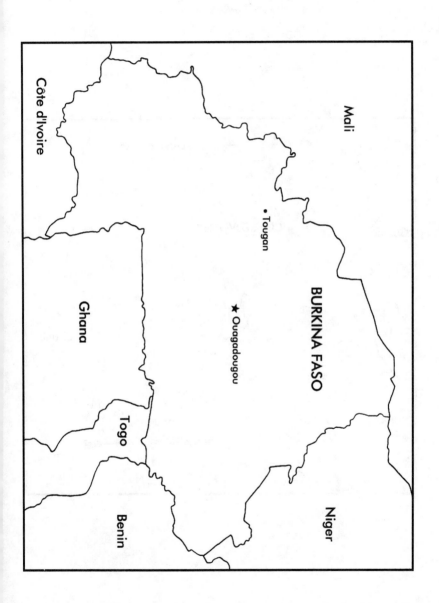

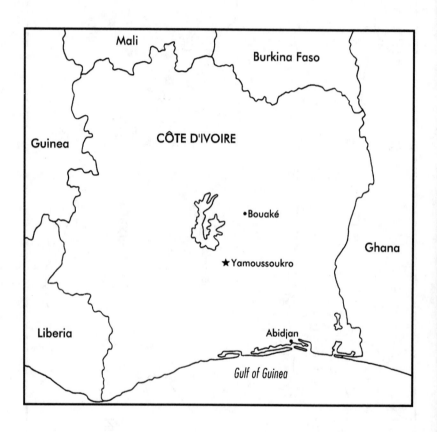

Contents

Foreword

During my lifetime I have met many people who have impacted my life in many different ways, but I have never met a couple who made a difference in my life every time I had the joy of visiting with them. Herb and Jessie lived life on the edge. They never stopped to think of themselves when others were in need. They were truly servants in every part of their ministry.

Herb and Jessie were *loyal friends*. I first met them while they were serving as dorm parents at the International Christian Academy in Bouaké, Côte d'Ivoire. They demonstrated their caring nature as they took my family in as if they had known us forever. During the time our careers overlapped in Burkina Faso they supported us in every way. While serving as field director I found them always to be there when I needed them. We traveled together, we lived together, we prayed together, we cried together. They knew the real meaning of friendship.

Herb and Jessie were *people of prayer*. The first time I visited them in the town of Tougan, where they served for many years, they were meeting with a dozen people under a straw shelter. They were not discouraged because they believed that God was going to do something special. They began a New Life for All program of evangelism. They bathed the program and the people in prayer, and God began doing exceptional things such as healings, conversions and other miracles. Everyone involved in the program began praying for his neighbors by name. God gave the increase.

Herb and Jessie were *generous people*. They gave to everyone who had need. A drought devastated the area where they were serving, and they responded by beginning an holistic ministry to address the food and water needs of the people. Jessie ministered to the sick who came in great numbers to her back door. Herb ministered to thousands by having wells dug and trucking in thousands of tons of grain to feed starving people. They never failed to share what God gave them.

Herb and Jessie were *people of faith*. They trusted God, and He answered over and over again. They loved to share their faith. Jessie never treated a patient without sharing the gospel with him. Herb shared the gospel all over Burkina Faso. They saw more Muslims come to Christ than anyone I know. Churches were needed in the Tougan District. Because of the Nehlsens' faith, God brought in the needed supplies. Tougan was a Muslim town with no interest in the gospel. Because of their faith the church grew from a straw shelter to a medium-sized church to a large church. They believed that when people pray God answers. They practiced it daily.

Herb and Jessie were *people of passion*. As I traveled with them in Guinea and in Burkina Faso, they would often cry over lost people. While in the United States on home assignment they were mission mobilizers. I have talked to many pastors who have reported that the ministry of the Nehlsens in their churches made a difference among their people. Their lives demonstrated their joy in Christ, and their actions demonstrated how much they loved Him.

The Nehlsens were special missionaries who made a difference in my life. I hope as you read this book that you will see how Christ used them to plant His Church in Burkina Faso and impact people around the world. God energized them to spread His glory.

Rev. David L. Kennedy
Assistant Vice President
Division of International Ministries
Colorado Springs, Colorado
August 14, 2001

1

Heading North

I had to laugh when they drove into the yard. They had said they'd arrive just before 8 a.m. Sure enough, it was 7:55 when the diminutive French car rolled to a stop, with Jessie's smiling face peering out the little half-window.

"You parked down the street just so you could arrive exactly precisely on time," I said, trying to be serious.

She laughed and denied it.

The two tall seniors unfolded themselves out of the aging Renault. In my heart I laughed again as they stood up. Nearly seventy-four and seventy-two respectively, Herb and Jessie Nehlsen looked pretty trendy considering the trip that lay ahead—Jessie in a full denim skirt with a flowered tee-shirt, and Herb decked out in jeans, a cotton shirt, fanny pack, baseball cap, sunglasses and comfortable-looking sports shoes.

Their excitement was palpable. This trip back to Tougan (TOO-gon) was a significant event to them. You see, Herb and Jessie had spent nearly forty years in Africa, most of them in the Tougan region of

Burkina Faso, as missionaries of The Christian and Missionary Alliance. Although they had officially retired in 1992, they were now doing a fifteen-month stint back in Africa helping their son, Steve, and his family in Côte d'Ivoire. Those fifteen months were almost over. Jessie and Herb would soon be heading back to retirement in North Carolina—at least that was the plan. However, as time had proven repeatedly, little in the life of the Nehlsens was ever predictable—except their arrival times!

My husband, Ron, and I were living in Africa too, in the same city as the Nehlsens. Getting to know this colorful pair had been a delight. It was Ron who encouraged me to seize the moment and write their biography for the Jaffray Series. Taking his advice, I had already started my research into what was increasingly unfolding as an amazing career. And so I too was eager to make the dusty trek north to where Herb and Jessie had spent so many productive years.

It was all working out smoothly. Ron and I had a trip to Burkina Faso already planned, so it made sense to include a visit to the Tougan area at the same time. And since Herb and Jessie wanted to say good-bye to their Tougan friends, it was decided we'd make the trip together. That was why we four were loading up the car that sunny Monday morning in 1999. The trip of about 500 miles would take us north through Ivory Coast (Côte d'Ivoire) and then into Burkina Faso. The first day would feature relatively painless travel on narrow but fairly decent paved roads.

As we loaded the car, I imagined Herb and Jessie looking somewhat askance at our shiny new mid-size

Peugeot station wagon. In their day, missionaries didn't drive cars like that. They were no doubt wondering too where on earth we would put all the grain, boards, African travelers, food supplies and cement we'd need to haul in order to do missionary work as they used to do!

But ever cheerful, these two upbeat people must have swallowed their doubts about a younger generation (us) as they stowed their matching suitcases into the back of the station wagon. Herb produced a good-sized bag of tracts and Gospels of John, which he tucked into the pouch by his seat. Then he and Ron climbed into the front, and Jessie and I claimed the backseat like the two meek and submissive women we are.

We prayed and asked for God's protection on the long road to Tougan, and then we were off. We were barely outside the city when Herb started talking, and, oh my, the stories that flowed as we drove along! I thought to myself, *Each of these stories is revealing what's important to him, some facet of his personality, character and spiritual gifting.*

The first one was about a little car just like his own which was in mint condition and was being sold locally for "a song." "I thought maybe I should buy it myself," he continued. "I always hated to pass up a good deal. There's always someone who would buy it."

Yes, I thought to myself, *that's vintage Herb. Always thinking, always looking for a deal, always seeing ways to make money. How can he still have so much entrepreneurial energy after all these years?* And I knew too where his profits would go; they would be ploughed back into helping some poor African friend with a pressing need. This was a man with the gift of helps if I'd ever seen one.

"You know," he laughed as we sped along that morning, "we hadn't been back in Africa too long this time before church leaders in the Tougan area sent us a list of eleven projects. Eleven! They wanted us to help them with metal roofs for some churches and to repair the president's motor bike. And in one village they have a really poor quality of mud. It wouldn't make durable bricks, so they had to make cement bricks. Well, cement is an awful lot more expensive than mud, so they needed help."

"And what did you do with that list of eleven projects?" I asked, knowing that we were likely talking about thousands of dollars.

"Well, it was really neat how it worked out," the big man up front explained, his broad face beaming. "Our friend, Ilo, a chauffeur by trade, needed a new vehicle; his was completely shot. So we liquidated some of our retirement savings, and we drew up a plan where most of the money would go to get Ilo a new bus. Then when he starts making money again, he'll pay that money back to the church leaders in installments and then they can finish up those eleven projects one by one."

Neither Ron nor I verbalized what we were thinking: *He surely didn't have any obligation to take care of any of those projects, much less all eleven of them. But he didn't seem to think that way. His beloved friends had needs, they came to him, and now it was natural for him to find a solution for them. The gift of helps, yes, but maybe a gift of mercy too?* I made a mental note to check for signs of unhealthy financial dependency on the Nehlsens when we got to Tougan. Would we find a significant missiological gaffe or two, given Herb's tender heart and open hand?

Meanwhile, Herb kept on chatting, and Ron kept on driving as we followed the narrow highway leading us north toward Burkina Faso.

When North Americans think about Africa they often picture lush rain forests or the savannah grasslands of safari fame or maybe vast expanses of golden desert. What we were seeing as we reached the most northern part of Côte d'Ivoire didn't fit any of those stereotypes. Instead, this was lightly forested country which was changing into village-dotted grasslands boasting trees which were getting progressively smaller and more scarce.

Eventually Jessie and I wanted to find a rest room, so we stopped at a Baptist hospital to make use of their facilities. Despite the fact that this was an unscheduled stop, before we had driven off that property Herb had talked to a staff member about the possibility of one of his young friends working there someday, tried to phone a hospital worker he knew and agreed to take letters to mail in Burkina.

As we drove away, I mused silently, *That's the difference between Herb and everybody else. His whole life is one big interaction with people and situations, and most often those situations are ones where he is actively trying to help out in some way.*

The road unrolled like a ribbon before us, and soon we had arrived at the border between Côte d'Ivoire and Burkina Faso. What surprised me was that there were no fewer than eight different checkpoints on this stretch of road. Each stop showcased the same drama. Ron would stop, and Herb, with passports, tracts and car documents in hand, would get out and approach the officers manning the post.

The scenario became predictable. Herb would get to the men, say something, extend his hand, and suddenly there'd be smiles all around—smiles and chit-chat and the occasional belly laugh. In short order a grinning Herb would be back saying things like, "He said he knew me from Tougan," or "That man said he used to play with my son, Steve, in Tougan."

Other times, when the car approached a barricade, from the backseat I'd see the corner of his eye start to wrinkle. And there he'd sit, making eye contact, smiling. As we rolled to a stop, out would go his big hand waiting to grasp the more reluctant hand of the man in charge of the spike belt blocking our way.

It all reminded me of a story Doloris Burns Bandy had told me about Herb. Tom, her husband, was recovering from a gallbladder attack and wasn't up to driving the long arduous trip to Kankan, especially with the rainy season approaching. He was field director at that time, and the men were going for a committee meeting.

African protocol dictates that one always goes through a third party when doing official business, presenting a gift, etc. It is the height of respect. It also brings in a witness for negotiations.

Herb offered to drive for Tom on this trip. It was a time of political unrest with many police and customs checkpoints along the way. The countries had just become independent of France and were "enjoying" their newfound officialdom.

At each stop Herb stepped out and greeted the uniformed policeman. He would ask Herb, "Do you have anything to declare?" Herb would respond, "I'll ask *le grand patron* [French for 'important boss']." Herb proceeded to the other side of the Jeep and asked Tom, "Patron, do you have anything to declare?" No, came the answer. Herb returned to the officer and said, "The patron says we have nothing to declare." This same dialogue and scenario was repeated for each of the many questions and at every stop.

Jessie had her own way of making our long trip enjoyable. She had made sandwiches with her good nay, *great* homemade rolls; these we munched as we rolled along. By the time we pulled into the town of Banfora, all we really wanted was a cold drink and a clean bathroom. We found both Dave and Denise Golding, Alliance missionaries from Vernon, British Columbia. But we found more than drinks and a bathroom. Dave, a former mechanic, offered to loan us his meticulously maintained and carefully driven Toyota Hilux in anticipation of the poorer roads we'd face up ahead. This vehicle exchange was a major act of faith on his part, and we were touched by his generous gesture. Not every mechanic of his ilk would consider loaning his vehicle, particularly with the knowledge of the kind of roads to which it would be subjected.

After transferring our luggage from the Peugeot into the Goldings' Hilux, we were once again heading north.

2

Wholesale Herb

The last lap of the day was soon behind us, and the city of Bobo Dioulasso (BO-bo ju-LA-so), or Bobo, as its often called, lay straight ahead. This vibrant, bustling city is home to Burkina Faso's Christian and Missionary Alliance headquarters where Herb and Jessie had spent the last two years of their Burkina career. The Mission station, only a decade old, was a welcome sight with its buildings painted in warm earthen tones, the driveway of rusty red shale and rows of towering trees offering welcome shade from the piercing afternoon sun.

An oasis to the four of us, the director's house, though not air-conditioned, seemed cool as we sat down to a round of frosted drinks and happy conversation with Doug and Karen Conkle. Knowing that we would be stopping over in Bobo, Karen had invited all the Alliance personnel living nearby for dinner. Before long they started to arrive: translator Mary Crowgey, bookkeeper/nurse Jetty Stouton, the crowd from Maranatha Bible Institute—Mark and Jeddie Brumley, Gretha Stringer, Lammert and

Britta Hukema, plus Adrie de Vroome who was visiting from another town. Later, sitting up to bowls of couscous and sauce arranged on a pink-and-green checked tablecloth, we chatted the evening away.

When the last of the strawberry shortcake had disappeared, we moved to softer chairs, and we four visitors were asked to "share." Jessie covered the news of their four children in her accurate, organized and unembellished fashion. Then it was Herb's turn. I wondered what he would say. Would he reminisce about their many years in Africa? Would he laud the old ways and doubt the new? Would he go on and on in garrulous disregard of the passing time?

To my delight, he did none of that. He didn't even mention the past, but launched into a passionate account of his and Jessie's current concerns for the Muslims with whom they were living and working. Part of his speech concerned the needs of converts whose families shun them because of their faith in Jesus. His compassion was compelling, and I thought, *That's Herb, the father, ever taking care of people.*

Before the crowd dispersed that evening, I was amused to glance across the room and see big Herb leaning over, removing his oversize sports shoe and showing some curious soul the magnets he wore under his insoles. Evidently, at least according to Herb, they improved some vital aspect of his health and well-being. The magnets, one of his daughter's businesses, were something in which he believed and promoted at every turn. *What an interesting person,* I thought, *always thinking and always positive and always a people person.*

I knew a legend of sorts had grown up around Herb there in Burkina Faso. Many people referred to him as "Demi-gros" (demi-grow). In English that means "wholesale" and everyone who knew Herb understood why that had become his moniker. Herb never bought just one of anything; he always bought huge quantities—cases of goods—especially when he found a good deal.

Herb really shone when he and Jessie had come out of retirement to oversee the dining room at a school for missionary children (May–July, 1997). He was absolutely in his element there, ordering cases of this and that and scouring the city for irresistible deals. And then he'd get behind the counter and ladle out food for the kids, as much as they could eat. The MKs remember him putting leftover desserts on a tray and going table to table trying to find somebody who could put away yet another dessert. He loved ice cream and would often supervise the kitchen help as they turned the cranks on three large freezers. He would then offer heaping bowls to the kids, who could hardly believe their good fortune.

Another time, in Burkina, when he was going into town for supplies, a pastor asked him to find an alarm clock. Herb found a store selling alarm clocks and counted their stock—twelve clocks. He bought them all! He figured if one pastor needed an alarm clock, then likely others did too. A friend of his said, "Every time we were with him he was always making purchases or getting bargains in big quantities 'because someone might need it.' " He'd come back from major shopping trips and sell the bargains he had found.

He'd even sell things he had purchased for their own needs! If you wanted it, you got it!

After one trip, when he returned loaded to the hilt, Jessie ruefully looked at the piles of supplies he had collected and said in her wry Scottish way, "Well, I have to say I sure did marry a good provider!"

While the good provider and his providee were sleeping across the hall that night, my own sleep was interrupted as I wheezed and sneezed, an allergic reaction to something in the room. Later, the Muslim call to prayer broke the early morning peace. The singsong voice coming from the mosque's loudspeaker droned on and on and on. But Herb and Jessie slept like babies and were raring to go when it came time to pull out of the yard.

We were no longer four passengers, but five, since Herb and Jessie's young friend, Anne, was going the rest of the way with us. Herb confided in me later that this winsome girl, daughter of his former yardman, was going to finish university in Mali and then go into nurses' training. There were two nursing school options. He was going to pay for the better one and then help her get a job. He kept repeating what a good girl she was and how much she loved the Lord.

But that wasn't the only story I heard as we drove along that sunny morning. The night before, a group of women had come to greet Jessie. As the bumpy miles passed beneath our wheels, Jessie rehearsed the memories their visit had triggered.

In 1990, she said, they had just moved to Bobo so Herb could be field director. True to her evangelist's heart, often in the afternoon Jessie would invite another lady to go around the neighborhood visiting and sharing her faith. One woman, Hawa, listened to her but said she really couldn't become a Christian because her husband would surely be opposed. Jessie had said, "But if you turn your life over to God, He'll use *you* to work in your husband's life, and he too could become a Christian."

Hawa didn't say much after Jessie prayed and took her leave. But now, eight years later, Hawa had come to tell Jessie the good news that she had indeed asked Jesus into her life. Later, through her, her husband had also become a Christian. "Now we're all Christians," she beamed, "except for my sister." This story reminded me of Jessie's pocket! The day before, I had seen her rifle through her pocket looking for something. She pulled out a wordless book. When she saw me watching her, she explained that she often carries a wordless book with her when she's traveling in case she has an opportunity to talk to children along the way.

As noon approached, we were getting close to the village of Poundou and what for Herb and Jessie would be a great delight. Herb told us that there was a Bible school at Poundou, and that a close friend, Emmanuel, a teacher there, had invited us for lunch. His wife, Rachel, was one of "Jessie's girls." Jessie had watched her grow and had taught her when she was in the girls' school near Tougan. We found out later that Herb and Jessie had also helped to arrange this couple's marriage when Rachel was just fifteen.

Following a dirt track, we turned off the main road into another world. There in the middle of nowhere stood an expansive community (maybe the size of two or three football fields) featuring rows of student housing, neat classrooms, a large chapel and two new houses for teachers, along with assorted other buildings both large and small. All of it was tidy, well-maintained and very plain.

We were there only an hour, but we learned a lot about this unique school. Arjo and Adrie de Vroome were giving support to this venture, and their Dutch efficiency was obvious everywhere. The Christian and Missionary Alliance (C&MA) of Holland and CAMA Services had channeled funds into this Bible school started by the national church, not by missionaries. In addition to that help, Arjo told us that the ninety students came with their own food and then paid tuition to the tune of less than $50 for a couple for one school year. National churches and the Mission also chipped in to contribute to the annual school budget and needs.

With that help and with students' planting fields and raising livestock, the school was able to function and support four Burkinabé teachers. The teachers' wives taught in the women's school and also helped Adrie in the dispensary. Bible schools are never cheap to run, but this one seemed to be doing an exceptionally good job of moving toward self-sufficiency. I wished we could have stayed longer to poke around in all the corners, but lunch was waiting at Rachel and Emmanuel's house.

Herb and Jessie ate the local food with their fingers just like their hosts. Ron and I chose spoons and considered ourselves lucky that rice and meat sauce were on the menu. The *toh*, pronounced "toe," cornmeal mush served in enamel bowls, and thick green gumbo Jessie and Herb were eating must have been, well, an acquired taste. They ate with great gusto and then both proclaimed themselves pleased with the menu and satisfied to boot!

Fortified physically, we once more consigned ourselves to the trusty Hilux for the rest of the trip.

3

Like a Horse Heading for the Old Barn Door

By 1:30 we were back onto the red and rutted trail that passed for a road up there in rural Burkina Faso. Herb's driving was punctuated with numerous "Man, this road is horrible" kind of comments. The dusty road did indeed offer quite a variety of negative features—deep holes, hardened tracks, washboard-like surface, powdery dust—to name a few. But every once in a while Herb would be able to shift into fourth gear, and we'd cruise along thanking the Lord for the comfort of the air-conditioned truck. At 14:20 (2:20) we pulled into the little city of Dédougou (day-DOO-goo).

"From here on I always divide the trip into three parts," Herb explained. "Twenty miles to what used to be called the Black Volta River, then another twenty miles to Sourou (SU-ru) where we first lived, and then a final thirty klicks into Tougan. But once we get to the river, we're already home—we're in Samogo country."

By the time we spied the bridge spanning the Black Volta, we were all pretty sick of the trip. Herb told us that Burkina has three rivers of note—the Black Volta, the Red Volta and the White Volta—and that eventually all of them merge, forming the Big Volta. It then continues down to Ghana where a large dam turns the river's force into electrical power. (The Volta names were, of course, all changed when the name of the country changed to Burkina Faso in 1984.)

Whoever made the bridge over the Black Volta River seemed to value height. We zoomed up, up and over, trying to ignore the missing guardrails on both sides of the narrow bridge spanning the rather modest river below. Then, with the Black Volta behind us, we were into the second third of the last lap to Tougan.

We passed through Zaba, a small village with an interesting story. It was obvious the village was prosperous and had had infusions of foreign money and technology. There was an impressive water tower, a significant grouping of solar panels and a sprawling, well-maintained mission station. Herb explained that in the olden days the Catholics wanted to set up a mission in the village of Sourou, but the official in charge of handing out those kinds of permissions happened to be a Protestant and noted that the Protestants had already requested this land. He refused the Catholic request and gave Sourou to the Protestants, a.k.a. The Christian and Missionary Alliance, and gave Zaba to the Catholics.

Herb and Jessie remembered when they first settled in Sourou back in 1956. They had moved into an
already established mission station, and Jessie immediately lent a hand at the nearby dispensary
where missionary nurse Emma (Wooledge) Orcutt
was waiting to show her the ropes. An experienced
African nurse, John, was also at work.

As we approached the little village, Herb and
Jessie looked this way and that, saying things like,
"When we lived here, those houses weren't there."
And "Oh, my! The roof is halfway off our house!"

Curious to see any remaining vestiges of Jessie and
Herb's presence in their first African post, we parked
the truck and walked around the station. The simple
church—they say seventy-five adults still worship
there every Sunday—was closed and locked that Tuesday morning. The dispensary, with its hideous white
and yellow coat of peeling paint, was apparently still
functioning, too, now staffed by a government nurse
and midwife but without adequate supplies and medicines. It was meeting only basic needs. A government
dispensary in the next village took care of the rest.

But the Nehlsens' house! Half the roof was gone,
likely as a result of violent windstorms that are so prev-
alent at the beginning and end of each rainy season.
The house was obviously no longer worth repairing.
Faded political symbols were painted across the front.
Herb explained that during Burkina's war with Mali
the church had reluctantly agreed to house military
personnel there and the military had painted those
signs. But now, an old Alliance pastor lived in the part
of the house that still had a roof. We could only hope

the church people would someday build him a better house.

Herb and Jessie recognized the old man, Pierre, who was coming toward us. As the Nehlsens stepped down from the truck, we witnessed a scene we'd see repeated many times in the next few days. Incredulous stares. Smiles of pure delight. Loud cries of pleasure. And then the hugging would start. Both men and women hugged both Herb and Jessie. There'd be a hug, then they'd pull back, take a look at the aging missionaries, and then another big hug with exclamations of surprise and joy. It was touching indeed to watch. I began to understand the love and veneration the people of this area had for the Nehlsens.

The pastor's family dragged a few locally made chairs out into the yard for us, but Jessie couldn't sit down. She walked around the yard with the pastor's wife, drinking in dimly remembered details of her very first African home. I found the whole place a bit depressing. Nothing there reminded me of the Herb and Jessie I knew. On the bright side, however, Christ's Body, numbering seventy-five or more, was there in all its redemptive power. Herb and Jessie's mission—to nurture this little group—had been accomplished, and now it was up to Pastor Pierre to continue the shepherding role.

An older woman quickly collected a bag of eggs and insisted that Jessie accept them. A gift of eggs is very African. A gift, to have maximum significance, has to be living. To the Africans, eggs fall into that category, and so this was an important gift of love from some very poor people to their beloved missionaries.

It was a relief when Herb said we should move along. As we climbed back up into the truck, I wondered why the Mission had settled in Sourou in the first place and then why the hardworking Nehlsens had relocated to Tougan after investing six precious years in Sourou. I looked forward to learning the answers to these questions. As the friends of Sourou waved us on our way, Herb once more took the wheel.

"Remember how I said the trip could be divided into thirds from that last big town? Well, we're into the final third now, and I always divide this last third into three sections too. I've always thought dividing the trip up this way made it go so much faster. In seven kilometers we'll come to a village, then in another ten there's another village, and at the end of the third distance of ten kilometers, we're there—we're at Tougan!"

We jolted and jerked along, and Herb laughed.

"Its funny. The car always goes faster when it's approaching Tougan," he commented with a smile. I thought of the proverbial horse heading for the old barn door, but this time it was Herb who was galloping home over the rough and rocky terrain.

We could feel it. Herb's excitement was growing, but Jessie kept her pleasure quietly tucked inside. We swayed and lurched through the first village, then a second. Sunbaked ruts scarring the road's dirt surface held the powerful truck back in third gear and oftentimes, second. As the late afternoon sun started sinking in the west, we heard the welcome words, "There, you can see the edge of Tougan now."

Tougan at last! The dusty town, unimposing in every way, passed before us until there—the Mission station lay straight ahead. Slowly Herb drove past the dispensary and then carefully eased the Hilux through the gate into a large enclosure outlined and shaded by multiple rows of towering trees. Journey's end!

Many Mission stations in Africa seem to have both the church and pastors' (or missionaries') houses built on the same tract of land, but that is not the case in Tougan. The Nehlsens' home was the equivalent of eight long city blocks away from the church. So on this day, the pastor and church people hadn't yet realized that Herb and Jessie had arrived because they were waiting at the church, not here at the house. Even so, a small but enthusiastic crowd surrounded us as we pulled into the yard. Herb and Jessie glowed as they greeted people whom they hadn't seen for at least eight years.

There was Jacques, their former yardman and gardener, along with Lydie, his wife, now an informally trained nurse, some of their children and assorted neighborhood folk. Once again, I saw the look of love in their dark eyes as they held Herb and Jessie close and wept tears of joy. Greetings over, we spent the next few hours settling into the Nehlsens' nearly empty house and exploring the spacious yard. No house looks great after it has sat empty for a while, and this one was no exception. But it was relatively clean, and I could easily picture Jessie reigning as queen of the kitchen now deprived of both refrigerator and stove.

Jacques, the yardman, had borrowed four single beds from somewhere and, wonder of wonders, both power and water were functional. The four of us could be comfortable there in "the house that Herb built," a house so full of memories for Jessie and Herb.

I was surprised to see a fireplace in the corner of the living room.

"Oh, yes, we were glad for that," Jessie explained. "In the cool season, around December and January, it would get plenty cold at night and in the morning, sometimes even down in the low 50s." It was anything but cold this night. Thankfully though, we noticed Jacques had found a fan for the Nehlsens' bedroom. We hadn't been in the house long before Jessie came into our room carrying the fan.

"You have it," she said, always a mother, always a giver.

As we meandered through the yard, Herb told us story after story. "Yes, that's my last windmill; I brought two of them from the U.S. over the years. And this is the water tower I built before the town had water." He showed us all the trees he and Jessie had planted. "Folks said we went overboard and planted too many and too close to the house. But trees make such a difference. Since they protect from both the sun and the winds, we planted 200 of them when we built this house."

He planted 200 trees! The scope of the tree-planting project is surely in complete harmony with his "wholesale Herb" image, I mused as we stood in the shade of those very trees, now tall and majestic. Some were fruit trees. Herb showed us one special mango tree whose fruit, he said, "was the closest thing to a peach you'd ever find."

Almost hidden among the trees was the old trailer "Pop" Martin, their predecessor, had bequeathed to Herb and Jessie. It was that old-fashioned kind, loosely resembling the shape of an egg, which boasted just two small windows on each side and one at each end. I tried, but failed, to imagine the six Nehlsens crammed into that little structure for itinerating in the villages.

"And there's the house I built for my yardman," Herb said, pointing to the left. Jacques' house was surrounded by signs of relative prosperity—a donkey and cart, chickens, goats. And behind his house sat the remains of the Nehlsens' beloved Starcraft holiday trailer given them by the Monticello, Minnesota Alliance Church.

"The wood inside is all rotted now," Herb observed, "but, my, that made a comfortable hotel when we were in the bush. It even had an inside toilet and a shower, which made things so much easier." I was glad Herb appreciated the trailer but thought to myself that no trailer, or local house for that matter, would ever be really comfortable for this big man.

"You see," Herb said, "when we moved to Tougan in 1963 there wasn't much here, and we had to do everything. The town was much smaller then, and there weren't any services available. So I had to have my own tools. In fact, the local mechanic came to borrow my tools to repair a car. And the town postmaster came once too. He had run out of stamps and knew I kept a good supply on hand, so he asked me to loan him some to sell until he could get more from the city!" Wholesale Herb had even kept the local post office afloat in those early days!

Jessie's breezeway dispensary surprised me. I knew her to be a meticulous and somewhat reserved woman, and so I found it difficult to imagine her wanting hordes of sick people just outside her kitchen door. *What about germs, and what about privacy?* I wondered. But I knew the answers to those questions even as they formed in my mind. This was a woman who from childhood had been intent on becoming a missionary. From what I could tell, the flame of faith lit in her childish heart had only grown brighter as the years had passed.

Jessie had one focus—her utmost for His highest. And if that meant interruptions during family times or unpleasant sights and smells on her very doorstep, so be it. She was ready and willing to sacrifice whatever was necessary to see "souls saved." Her breezeway, a simple cement structure, suddenly seemed a hallowed place that afternoon. We were standing on holy ground.

4

The Mother of All Reunions

Night was falling, and Jacques, the yardman, told us that the church people were getting ready to host us over at the church. Since the meal wasn't ready quite yet, Ron took the opportunity to have a nap while Jessie and I read, perched on straight-backed chairs. And Herb? There he was, hunched over the table with his English Bible open beside his Jula Bible. It was hard to tell which Bible looked more worn.

"They want me to speak to the pastors tomorrow," he explained simply.

It was pitch black outside—that black equatorial darkness—when someone came to say that the meal was ready and the pastors were waiting for us. We drove to the church. As Ron and I stepped out of the truck, we couldn't see a thing! But out of the darkness arose the now-familiar cries as one after another of the older pastors recognized their beloved missionaries. Into the beam of the headlights they came until we could see them clutching Herb and Jessie in their arms. The deep darkness surrounding the church hid almost everything, but not the shiny white teeth gleaming as joyful church elders led the Nehlsens toward a small dormitory off to one side.

There, on a rough wooden table in front of the narrow building, sat two gigantic metal tubs faintly illuminated by the light coming from the dormitory's windows and doors. With visions of toh and gumbo dancing through my head, I blessed the all-encompassing darkness on our side of the table and resolved to take very little, to eat next to nothing, and then to hide my plate under other plates to disguise my culinary cowardice.

However, with sinking heart I noticed some of the younger pastors wrestling with a portable fluorescent light which they finally plugged in, bathing the ominous pots in dismaying clarity. My heart sank. My stomach churned, but only briefly—for help was on the way. Within seconds, swarms of loud and aggressive insects rushed toward the light. The pastors reluctantly removed the offending tube, and in the darkness this meat-and-potatoes girl breathed a fervent prayer of thanksgiving while deeply admiring Herb and Jessie for their commitment to the local cuisine, so different from traditional Western fare.

We took our places on the backless benches around the table. Directly across from us was the highest-ranking church leader in that region, Rev. Jacques Toni. He was an old man, and two of his tall sons, pastors, were also there. Herb had told us of his humility and of the respect he enjoyed from other pastors. He also explained that in a shake-up when the national church president stepped down, Pastor Jacques had retained his post as vice-president.

One of the pastors thanked the Lord for the food and then handed Jessie two big dippers with which to dish out the food.

"Give me the tiniest amount possible," I whispered, "and just sauce. No solids, please." However, to my delight, the plastic dish contained only rice and chicken sauce, not the gumbo and toh of my earlier nightmares.

In the chitchat which followed as everyone was served, Herb said, "They're speaking their own language; they always do when they talk among themselves." I knew he spoke Jula, the trade language, and I asked him how much of their own dialects he understood. He replied that he could follow the gist of a conversation if he knew the general topic being discussed. *How difficult it must be to do nearly forty years of missionary work and see a church district grow from two pastors to over eighty pastors while communicating through a trade language, and not the people's mother tongue,* I mused. It was hard to reconcile the things I was seeing—the deep love shown to Herb and Jessie and the linguistic distance which must have always been a part of their relationships.

Later, back at the house, we couldn't help but notice the nearly deafening din of hundreds of humming insects and the total blackness outside unrelieved by so much as a single street light. But sleep came quickly to the four of us, and by dawn's light we were ready to take a tour of Jessie and Herb's beloved Tougan.

The first thing we saw that morning, though, was Jessie at her finest. At the prettiest spot in the house, the veranda, she had laid out her own homemade cinnamon bread. I knew Jessie was famous for her hospitality, and it was not hard to understand why as we watched her preside ever so regally over a simple breakfast served on napkins for lack of plates. In a true spirit of unity, the four of us took turns using the only two knives we had.

As we sipped Jessie's coffee, Herb told us how he had built this house for $4,000 back in the '60s. "The Mission said if we wanted a screened porch it would be at our personal expense—the Mission wouldn't pay for it." He went ahead and built it anyway. It became their favorite eating spot and even a sensible sleeping option during the hottest months. During those sweltering days, when the temperature often approached 120 degrees Fahrenheit and dropped to only 90 degrees at night, the porch at least allowed for some errant breezes to bring minimal relief.

This morning, any thoughts of lingering on the veranda were dashed as Herb and Jessie herded us back into the truck. Soon we were on our way down a road built by French Canadians back in the days when Herb was building the Tougan church. Stories of how these road builders ate Jessie's cooking and then helped Herb build the church were absolutely thrilling to hear, but a far bigger thrill lay just ahead.

In very short order we were entering a tiny village named Kassan. Burkina villages don't look like stereotypical African villages. From a distance you can't even see the village; all you see is a mud wall enclosing something. But you know it must outline a village because of the small herds of goats and sheep tended by ragged children wandering around the perimeter. Donkeys pulling carts to and from the walled area are another dead giveaway.

Inside the village, it soon becomes clear that the wall is actually a series of walls, joined together, enclosing individual courtyards. Each family grouping lives in one of these courtyards in a rectangular house covered by thatch or metal roofing. Other buildings include round granaries, usually slightly elevated, and shelters for various animals—donkeys, goats, sheep, cows, chickens. All these structures are made from the same sun-dried bricks of rusty brownish hue.

Kassan's mud wall, almost orange and nicely rounded on the top, offered few clues to what we were about to see. We drove around the circumference of a large area, following the mud-brick wall until we came to the enclosure's entrance. But this was no ordinary entryway—it was a classroom building. And beside it a group of youth were talking to an elderly man. When the villagers heard the truck, then saw who was in the cab, people started running toward us from every direction. Soon the now familiar cries of joy filled the air. Even Jessie wept as she saw the tears of happiness and the outstretched arms. Herb, of course, never bothered to hide his tears.

This school was run by elderly Pastor Paul and his wife, Rebekah. Jessie explained that church people in remote villages had little chance to educate their girls or prepare them for Christian marriages. So the early missionaries had established a school where teenage girls, under the tutelage of a pastor and his wife, would be taught reading, writing and Bible, as well as useful skills such as sewing and proper conduct. From the beginning of the school in this village Jessie had taught every Thursday. Although it was started as a school for teenage girls, running from September until December, it soon began to hold classes for young men from January until April every year.

"One year, when our son, Steve, was at St. Paul Bible College," Jessie said, beaming, "he came out with some other students to help build the Tougan church. We didn't have all the building permits in place yet, so rather than waste their time while awaiting the permits, those boys built that dormitory over there, even helping make the sun-dried bricks." She pointed out the pastor's house and the chapel which Herb and a men's team from Minnesota had built and the attractive classroom built by friends of the Alliance in Holland.

As we looked around, I felt various emotions welling up inside. The order and discipline of the place was strikingly evident. The dozen or so girls currently there were dressed modestly and behaved with maturity. Someone told me that a majority of pastors' wives in that region had passed through Kassan's school. *Is it any wonder,* I thought, *with this kind of character formation in women's lives that their pastor-husbands are famous for the number of their parishioners and for the spiritual progress of their region?*

The courtyard seemed quite prosperous. Donkeys, sheep and lots of fowl wandered freely (which made

walking about a bit hazardous). Pastor Paul too made
a profound impression on me. If I had to choose a
word to describe him, I'd pick an old-fashioned
word—faithfulness. There was a good reason for that.
Although we had arrived without warning and before
8 a.m. on a Wednesday morning, we found him already dismissing a Bible study for young men in the
village. This was a small school, behind courtyard
walls, out of sight of the rest of the region and the rest
of the world. Yet year after year after year, he kept on
faithfully doing the same thing: shepherding the flock
in Kassan.

Just before leaving, we all trooped into the chapel
and, while we four sat on homemade wicker recliners,
the others were seated on the cement benches which
Herb had installed when he built the church. Those
benches fascinated me. Being cemented to the floor,
they never got out of order, were never eaten by ter-
mites and had a shiny, silvery look to their well-worn
surfaces.

After forty-five minutes of listening to the girls'
choir sing, the local choir sing and an emotional
Herb speak a last word to his spiritual grandchildren,
we took a photo of the crowd and then were off, back
to Tougan—accompanied by two live chickens rest-
ing comfortably at Ron's feet. The chickens, gifts to
Herb and Jessie, were actually occupying a spot on
the truck floor where I was to put my feet. However,
not having learned discipline and submission at
Kassan's Girls' School, I hopped in the back beside
Jessie and left Ron to his fowl company.

Back to Tougan we went with happy hearts and a new window into Jessie and Herb's world of yesteryear. The next stop was to be at the Tougan church, the "miracle" church, but before arriving, we took care of a Herb-style idea. He thought the truck would ride better on the return trip if sacks of sand were loaded into the back. We were in favor of anything to promote a smoother ride, so we went along with his plan. This wasn't a new or novel idea, of course, but it was certainly a very "Herb" thing to do. Once again, I admired this resourceful man and his gift of helps.

On our way to the church, the Nehlsens wanted to show us Tougan's very first dormitory, a small, three-room mud-brick building. They explained that Christian families in outlying villages wanted to send their children to the government school in Tougan but needed a place for them to stay. Missionaries of Herb and Jessie's era would try to build dormitories and then find dorm parents to create a Christian home for these boys.

At the gate to the now-decaying courtyard, a handicapped believer was selling a primitive sort of string art to support himself. Herb encouraged us to buy some to help the man out. Then it was time to point the truck toward the church.

The church by daylight showed an entirely different face than its mysterious shadows of the night before. Throngs of pastors stood around the imposing structure, while off to the side a group of women sitting on little stools tended cooking pots in the outdoor kitchen. As the truck nosed its way past the cement walls surrounding the property and into the yard, the people thronged toward us. We had met a few pastors the night before, but this was the first time for most of this crowd to have a chance to greet Herb and Jessie.

Years before, back in the '60s when the district was starting to grow, the pastors had asked Herb to help them organize themselves. He recommended that they meet each month; teaching, fellowship and prayer one month, and then the next month the same thing plus any necessary business matters. The day of our arrival fell during one of those monthly meetings. It was a great opportunity to see and understand the spiritual health of this district as evidenced by all the pastors flocking around us.

Hugs, cries, handshakes, exclamations of delight— it was all happening again. The wizened old pastors, the virile younger men—they all looked alike to me. But to Herb and Jessie each one was a beloved friend, and it was evident that their love was reciprocated.

To one side of the church yard was the new, vastly improved and much larger dormitory, which housed boys and girls and replaced the ramshackle affair we had toured earlier. Lying at its entrance was a stout gray pig who had given his life for this occasion and was being skinned even as we tried to avert our eyes.

The old chapel Herb had first built there in Tougan stood off to the side, its granite face glistening in the distance. Glancing from the modest chapel over to the stately and spacious "new" church, I thought of all the years of blood, sweat and tears that had gone into this compound, from its small beginnings to the present prosperity. Herb's favorite expression, "Hallelujah anyhow," had stood him in good stead during those

years. He always said that even when things aren't going well, it's important to praise the Lord anyhow and
then watch as our living, loving God works everything
out for our good and His glory.

During the famine years starting in 1973, his big
heart had broken as he watched his beloved Samogos
suffer year after year. With tears, he told of at least being able to find some grain to help and being able to
sponsor work-for-food projects. With a voice choked
with emotion, he concluded, "We just really praise the
Lord." Brokenhearted? Yes. Discouraged? Not at all—
just praising the Lord for what He was doing in the
midst of disaster.

Herb's daughter, Debbie, said, "I never saw him
discouraged. Not once. He saw every problem as an
opportunity to trust God and see how God would
work it out." It made such an impression on her that
she once painted those words, "Hallelujah Anyhow,"
on a wooden plaque and gave it to her dad for his office wall.

Jessie told me, "When we first arrived in Africa, we
prayed, 'Lord, keep our hearts burdened, tender, caring that these people are lost.' " The Lord's answer to
that prayer had kept the Nehlsens there in the Tougan
region, through good times and bad, for nearly thirty-
five years. The result of that love was seen all around as
I looked from the little chapel to the crowd of pastors
milling around the yard and then over to the imposing
structure where the meeting was about to begin.

What others might call "the church that Herb
built," he called "the miracle church." In addition to
its size (3,000 square feet) the metal shutters, the

green metal doors, the high, high ceiling showing the steel girders supporting the roofing tins—all this was very attractive to the eye. But what defined the sanctuary were the rows of cement benches set in ever-widening semicircles around the pulpit— shiny, pearly gray benches that could never get shoved out of order, so pretty—and functional too.

We drove away later, leaving Herb and Jessie in the church surrounded by a crowd of Samogo pastors, eighty of them in all. It was a reunion no one would ever have anticipated back in 1956 when the Nehlsens first moved to Burkina Faso. A gathering of this magnitude could never have been realized without Jessie and Herb's lifetime of loving and hard work there in the Tougan region.

During their first year in Africa, Jessie and Herb had knelt together and prayed, "Oh, Lord, for Your name's sake, let us show these Samogo people a life of love. And let us live this life so clearly that everyone will see our love and will turn to You." God had answered that prayer. Herb always said, "We were the couple who could not sing, did not have any great gifts, but we asked God to give us a love for the people, which He did, and then we worked with what we had even though it wasn't much. But God—He did the rest." And so, for nearly forty years these two humble Americans spoke their own language, the language of love, loudly and clearly.

Is that why the Tougan area is spiritually strong today? Is that why there are more than eighty pastors working among the district's 220 villages today? Is that why no other church district outstrips this one in ongoing training in God's Word at both the re-gional and local church level? Is that also why the churches in the Tougan district have received solid training for their Sunday school workers?

Jessie, on her arrival, had been horrified to see what seemed to be a lack of concern for children's souls. This didn't sit well with her mother's heart or with her own early conditioning when she had watched her mother teach Bible clubs in her home. So she paid close attention as a missionary from Mali offered a training seminar for Sunday school teachers, and then she was off, offering seminars herself to Christians who wanted to be teachers.

One by one, villages became interested and sent someone for this bimonthly training. It became more and more popular as teachers understood the value of a child's soul and got excited about teaching children. Eventually this training moved into the hands of the national church leaders. Thanks to Jessie, today's children in the Tougan area have a far better chance of hearing the gospel in ways they can understand than they ever had before her arrival.

Ron and I, preparing to leave, looked around one last time at the crowd surrounding the Nehlsens. I realized what we were witnessing here was a gigan-tic, full-color snapshot of the lives of Herb and Jessie sitting on a stack of years full of preparation, family dramas, a lot of hard work—and love.

Jessie's life verse is Second Corinthians 2:14: "But thanks be to God, who always leads us in triumphal procession in Christ and through us spreads every-where the fragrance of the knowledge of him." As we now begin the chronological account of Herb and Jessie's ministry, we'll watch them take part in Christ's triumphal procession, and we'll see how God, through them, spread everywhere in the Tougan region the fragrance of the knowledge of Him.

5

Through Days of Preparation

It was during a Hi-Crusader Club meeting that teenaged Jessie Ewing of Villa Park, Illinois, met "a big happy guy who came to school with the biggest lunch box and the biggest sandwiches made from his mom's homemade bread." That big happy guy, Herbert Henry Nehlsen, had come into the world on February 28, 1926, in Oak Park, Illinois. The elder of two sons born to his Swiss-German mother and Danish-German father, Herb learned to work hard.

"I always had a job—selling newspapers, weeding and plowing gardens, cutting lawns—any odd job I could find." This pattern of working hard and looking for things to do would become a life pattern for Herb. He was also an achiever—president of his youth group, soul-winner and manager of the Wheaton basketball team for two years. He eventually earned two basketball letters.

Herb's walk with God started in his childhood when, without anyone praying with him, he made a decision for Christ. As a gangly teenager, he became an enthusiastic participant in the Hi-Crusader for Christ group, and it was there that he committed his life to the Lord and was filled with the Holy Spirit. At the age of eighteen, just after his graduation from high school, he joined the army and became a part of the mechanized cavalry.

On New Year's day, 1945, Herb was shipped overseas on the *Queen Mary*. Herb's captain volunteered his outfit, the 28th Infantry Division (Pennsylvania), to follow up General Patton on his drive across France and Germany. They crossed over the Rhine on the first American-built pontoon bridge and then moved into Germany to mop up and hold what Patton had taken. Although some of Herb's division were lost to land mines, his life was spared.

After the war, Herb's outfit was sent to Kaiserslautern, Germany, to wait for transfer to Japan. Since he had taken typing in high school, Herb volunteered to help in the office where the processing was being done. By his own admission, that kept him out of trouble and eventually led to a promotion to staff sergeant. This pattern of looking for things to do, volunteering, working hard and succeeding would typify his style in years to come.

He turned down an offer to stay in the army in favor of joining the Lord's army. His father had earlier said he would loan Herb money to go to Massachusetts Institute of Technology (MIT) where he had already been accepted. Herb's father thought preparing for the ministry was a waste of time, so he wouldn't help Herb go to Wheaton. But the Lord knew all about that. The GI bill paid most of his costs at Wheaton College. The rest were covered by various jobs, including summers working with a cement gang constructing forms and pouring foundations. There he earned a new nickname, The Great Dane, an allusion to both his ethnic background and his hefty physique.

One frosty morning, January 19, 1928, the Ewing family of Oak Park, Illinois, welcomed a new baby into their family, a second daughter. Although the father had hoped this baby would be a boy, the newborn daughter was given a significant name: she became the fourth Jessie, after her mother and both her Scottish grandmothers.

Baby Jessie and her older sister were joined seven years later by a brother. In this family of three children, Jessie grew up with a strong work ethic modeled all around her. Her dad took the train to work in Chicago every day even during the Great Depression, and her mom was always working too—teaching Sunday school, teaching neighborhood children in her own home and in other homes, and entertaining missionaries.

Jessie says, "We had one very special friend through my growing-up years who was a missionary in China with the South China Boat Mission. We were fascinated as she told us about living on a houseboat and going up and down the river telling people about Jesus. She adopted a little Chinese girl who had been rejected by her family and named her Jessie Mae after my sister and me!"

So it wasn't a big leap for Jessie to understand her personal need of a Savior and later to want to be a missionary. "My first and lasting memory of church was attending special meetings for children at our neighborhood Bible church and seeing the film *Christie's Old Organ*. In some way God touched my seven-year-old heart that night, and I remember crying and asking Jesus to forgive my sins. That was the day I was born into God's family."

Her mother had already become a Christian thanks to neighborhood women who had come to call and explain the way of salvation to her. When a few days after their visit Jessie's mother heard the same Good News on Moody Bible Institute's radio station, she knelt by her radio to invite Christ into her life. Jessie says of her parents, "Daddy was quiet about his faith, but I know he loved Jesus. Mother, on the other hand, was very active in sharing her faith with others."

Jessie had had childhood dreams of becoming a missionary, but in high school other things became important—having fun, someday getting a good job and eventually marrying a fine young man she hoped would be coming along soon. She took secretarial courses to prepare for that good job, and she did have a lot of fun. One highlight was attending a Hi-Crusader Club each Tuesday evening at her high school. This club, taught by Wheaton College students, turned out to be pivotal in her life and in the life of her future husband.

Although Jessie remembers lots of good times there, she also remembers that God spoke to her heart, so much so that in her third year of high school she finally asked Him what His plan was for her life. "I can remember realizing that I belonged to Him, and it was only right that He be the one to plan my future," she says. "I recommitted my life to God; wherever He would lead I would follow. This meant college, to prepare for whatever He had for me."

Herb and Jessie began college the same year, Herb an ex-GI, Jessie just out of high school. Both were preparing to serve the Lord in missions. Herb knew that he needed the mate that God had designed for him, and soon he was convinced that Jessie was that one. Jessie wasn't so sure. She dreamed of marrying a tall, dark and quiet man. Here was Herb, tall, yes, but blond and so outgoing.

Their romance was on and off, but toward the end of their sophomore year Herb finally stole Jessie's heart. But by then more changes were in store. Jessie knew that God was leading her away from college into nurses' training.

Herb tells how, in his senior year, he "almost blew it." After at last winning Jessie's heart, he began to be convicted that he was spending too much time with her and not enough at the rescue mission and working in a Sunday school he directed. Instead of talking this over with Jessie, he just broke up with her. But his heart soon told him he had done the wrong thing. He was so unhappy that he wanted to get as far away from her as possible! So he applied to Columbia Bible College Graduate School.

As Herb tells it, "Just before I left, my mother packed a lunch for me and suggested I take Jessie on a picnic. So I did. And that was the day a spark was fanned into a flame. A few months later when I came home for my brother's wedding, a special cousin gave me some good advice. 'It would be a good idea if you gave Jessie a ring so that others know she's taken.' " So in November 1950, that part of their future was settled. They would serve God together wherever He would send them. Only God knew how their gifts and abilities would complement one another in the years to come.

By the time they were married, Jessie had graduated from nursing school, and Herb had finished one year toward his master's degree. Together they continued to pursue their missionary dream. It seemed to them that many Missions were looking for specialists such as doctors and teachers and not for candidates called to church planting and evangelism. This perception finally led them to apply to a church-planting Mission, The Christian and Missionary Alliance. An interview with Dr. A.W. Tozer marked the beginning of the Nehlsens' lifetime involvement with the Alliance.

A year at Nyack College in New York was required for all missionary candidates. So Herb headed east to Nyack, leaving Jessie with her parents to await the arrival of their first baby. Beautiful Rebecca June arrived on September 24, 1952, at the hospital where Jessie had done her training. Two weeks later, little Becky took her first flight—to Nyack, to meet her proud father.

With God's enabling, Herb and Jessie managed the strenuous year that followed. Herb took eighteen credit hours at the college and also worked forty hours a week in a paper box factory. Jessie cared for their newborn and took two classes.

The next step was home service, an Alliance requirement before going overseas. It was at Deer Creek Chapel near Lorimor, Iowa, among loving farm people who kept them well supplied with eggs, milk and cream. They turned a country schoolhouse into a parsonage with a pump and a path—more primitive than their home in Africa would be!

In February of 1954, another beautiful girl, Deborah Ruth, was born, and Jessie and Herb received the long-awaited letter from the Mission's headquarters: "Nehlsens are assigned to Sourou, Upper Volta!" Herb and Jessie, with Becky and Debbie, were finally on their way to Africa.

When Jessie learned her missionary role would be overseeing a dispensary and maternity clinic, she left her little girls with their grandmothers and tackled a midwifery course in Philadelphia. Because of the fast-approaching departure date for language study in France, Jessie managed to cram a six-month course into just two months. She called it "a miraculous answer to prayer." Others would say it was her own hard work, determination and sacrifice which helped answer that prayer.

At that point, the Nehlsens' future was no more than a dream on the horizon. There was no thought of remuneration or retirement. They didn't even know what their monthly allowance was going to be.

All they wanted to do was to serve the Lord. For the next forty years Herb and Jessie would work and pray to make their dream a reality.

6

A Grim and Glorious Battle

Barely moving, the ship finally nudged against the battered quay. So this was Africa! At last, after an interesting and challenging year of language study in Paris, France, two eager and enthusiastic North Americans with their small daughters in tow stepped onto African soil for the first time. As Jessie and Herb strained to find at least one white face at the Abidjan port, they were filled with great faith, optimism and yes, some apprehension. They were ready to work, to laugh, to pray, to give their entire lives to the people of West Africa. They set their faces toward the unknown.

It was July of 1956. Big Herb, taller-than-average Jessie and the two Nehlsen girls, Becky and Debbie, crammed themselves into the Studebaker pickup next to John Johanson who had come down from Upper Volta to meet them. Packed in like the proverbial sardines, they navigated the never-ending red-dirt road north toward their new home in Sourou, Upper Volta. It was a three-day trip inland. The first day they

headed to Bouaké, the headquarters of the Côte
d'Ivoire Mission. The next day they drove to Bobo
Dioulasso, their Upper Volta headquarters. There
they purchased some necessary provisions for their life
"in the bush," not really knowing just what foods they
would need. As one dusty mile followed another,
Jessie found herself thinking of an old, familiar missionary song. It seemed her destination was indeed a
"region beyond" that seemed to be literally the end of
the earth. At the end of this long road was the Tougan
district, comprised of 220 villages. This young couple's
overwhelming assignment was to reach those villages
with the good news about Jesus.

Upper Volta, a small landlocked country about the
size of Colorado, is encircled by six other African
countries. In 1956 it boasted fewer than 6 million
people. There was a paucity of natural resources and
only a few cash crops—sesame seeds, cotton, livestock and peanuts—because in most places only a
thin layer of red dirt covered layers of laterite rock.
Located in what is known as the Sahel, the region
just south of the Sahara Desert, it had the dubious
distinction of being among the ten poorest countries
in the world. The average annual income? "A paltry
$156 U.S.," Herb would say, shaking his big head.
He'd then go on to relate a poignant story. It illus-
trated perfectly his African friends' concept of the
necessities of life, a concept worlds removed from
his own and even further removed from that of his
fellow Americans living in the United States.

When Timothy and his wife were attending Bible school, they were assigned to work in a vil-

lage, in a new church, for one year of practical training before graduating. Timothy said he wouldn't be able to go to that particular village.

Some thought he was afraid of taking a new church; others thought he just wasn't ready. They finally asked him why he couldn't accept the leadership of this new church plant. He replied that he'd always lived with his parents, even after his marriage, and he and his wife simply didn't have the necessities of life to start out by themselves.

Jessie and I asked what was lacking, and we found he didn't have a rope for the well with a rubber bucket on the end. Nor did he have a pail for water or the two cooking pots they needed. And they didn't have two bowls for eating either—one for corn mush and one for the gravy.

A rope, a dipper, a pail, two pots and two bowls. Those to him were the necessities of life, and he didn't have them or the money to buy them. Such was the poverty of Burkina Faso. However, with the help of the church committee, Timothy eventually got these "necessities of life" and started his ministry.

Jessie knew she wouldn't be that poor during her missionary life, but she also knew that she was in for some new experiences. For one thing, she had heard that she'd be living in a sun-dried mud-brick house. So, upon arrival in the town of Sourou, she was surprised and delighted to see the spacious white house that would be her home. Yes, it was made of mud, but the mud bricks had been plastered and then whitewashed, transforming the simple structure into an attractive, even homey, dwelling.

The house, recently vacated by veterans Pop and Helen Martin, already contained enough heavy wooden furniture so the new missionary family could settle right in. There was no electricity, of course, but they had running water thanks to a boy who pumped it from the well into a barrel. Another pump then sent the water to a higher barrel under the eaves from where it flowed down into the house.

The ceiling made of roofing tins and a roof made of the same metal formed an attic area which was ruled by a prolific and very malodorous bat population. Only serious feline attacks were going to decimate that crowd! So Herb formulated a strategy appropriate for the occasion. He propped a ladder against the wall, then taught a cat how to climb the ladder and hunt its dinner!

The tin roofing sheets were functional but not perfect. The first rains of the season descended, ushered in by terrifying windstorms. One day, with a burst of uncontrolled fury, the wind savagely attacked the Nehlsen home, ripping off half of the roofing tins. And then the torrential rain came crashing down. Damp, frightened and dismayed, the family huddled under what was left of the roof on one side of the house as other rooms flooded in the wake of the angry storm. There in the driest part of the house, Herb prayed while Jessie tried to shelter their little girls and a three-week-old orphan in their care. As the rain continued to fall in pelting sheets, the group even sang, and later, when the storm finally passed, a relieved Herb and Jessie counted their blessings. Yes, the whitewashed walls were streaked with mud, and a big repair job lay ahead of them. But they were all safe.

Their house was only a stone's throw from an old church built by earlier missionaries. Another stone's throw away was the dispensary where Jessie would go every day to lend a hand to John, the local nurse. Although the government had built the clinic, it had been given over to the Protestant Mission, a.k.a. The Christian and Missionary Alliance, to manage. Jessie viewed her nursing as giving a cup of cold water in Jesus' name. As she showed God's love through her actions, she also asked God to give her opportunities to tell her patients about the Great Physician who could heal their souls as well as their bodies.

Beside their medical work and starting to develop relationships with the Samogo people, language study was a formidable mountain before them, a veritable Everest. The San language was the mother tongue of the Samogos, but since it was an unwritten language with a difficult grammatical structure and several dialects, the more accessible Jula, the language of the traders, became Herb and Jessie's language study assignment.

The Mission's decision to assign the Jula language to Herb and Jessie ended up having far-reaching implications during their later years of ministry. For the present, however, language study just meant a tremendous amount of very hard work.

Mission leaders thought Jula study could best be accomplished by temporarily moving the young family to

Mali where they could be guided by veteran missionaries. "We are no linguists," Herb wrote home, "and
language study isn't fun, but we want to win this battle
so that we might go on into a bigger battle, the grim
and glorious battle for souls."

At the end of the hard years of language study, Herb
wrote to friends, "God has given us a son. Think of it, a
fine, healthy 7 pound 5 ounce baby boy, Stephen
James. Will you pray with us that Stephen will grow up
to be an instrument in the hands of the Living God?"
At that time, only God knew how He would abun-
dantly answer that prayer.

It soon became evident to Jessie that nursing in the
local dispensary was completely different from its
North American counterpart. Sometimes women having their eighth or ninth baby would wait too long before heading for the dispensary and would end up
delivering the child by the side of the road. When that
happened, they would arrive with the baby, complete
with placenta, in a gourd or basin carried on someone's head. Jessie would give the mother a good scold-
ing and a tetanus shot, then try to keep mother and
baby in the dispensary until the baby's umbilical cord
fell off.

Jessie often called on the Lord for wisdom in difficult deliveries; only once did she opt to take a patient
to the government hospital twenty miles away. That
woman had seemed unable to deliver, but curiously
enough the bumpy twenty-mile ride did the trick. She
delivered immediately upon arrival at the hospital.

Those were still colonial days, and France's African colonies received certain benefits from their co-

lonial masters, benefits such as French doctors to staff the government hospitals and medicines that were both free and plentiful. So when Jessie saw serious cases, such as hunting injuries where hands had been partly blown away by gunpowder, for example, she'd call Herb, the ever-willing chauffeur, and off the wounded would go for surgery at the government hospital. The more routine cases—intestinal parasites, burns, diarrhea, fevers of all sorts, and of course, childbirth—Jessie handled herself.

The people believed sickness was tied to the occult. They were certain that every sickness was caused by a curse; someone had put a curse on them. This demanded revenge—and poisoning was a common method of avenging a wrong. One opportunity to do that was when men were passing a gourd of beer around the circle. The victim of some bad luck would look for an occasion to flick a minuscule amount of poison out from under his thumbnail into the beer and then hand it on to the man suspected of cursing him. The potency of the poison usually meant eventual death for the suspect.

One time a man arrived at the Mission dispensary. Although his illness looked like severe constipation, Jessie learned that he had been poisoned. Since she knew he would soon die anyway, despite her best efforts, she decided to do nothing except ease his pain and pray that God's truth would free the dying man's spirit before it was too late.

Herb and Jessie sometimes inherited newborns when the mother did not survive childbirth. It was considered bad luck for another woman to nurse an orphaned baby, yet bottles weren't an option in that remote area. In fact, in the not-so-distant past, the baby would have been dropped into the grave with its mother. Although the French outlawed that practice, newborn orphans still presented a problem. The Nehlsens' door must have been perceived as a good spot to abandon a baby! Over the years, at least ten babies found love and nutrition in Jessie's arms until Herb could deliver them to a neighboring area where infertile Christian couples were happy to adopt them.

After three years at Sourou, the Nehlsens' own family was about to expand. Sadly, the eagerly awaited baby came too soon and lived only a few hours. Baby Stanley Nehlsen's arrival turned happy anticipation into the deep grief only a bereaved family can understand.

Shortly after the baby's death, an old African pastor arrived carrying a piece of white cloth for wrapping the tiny body. There in the yard, the old man himself dug the grave. A grieving Jessie wrote to family and friends, "It was a tremendous disappointment to us this month when the precious baby boy we 'had on order' was born two-and-a-half months prematurely on September 11, 1959. Our God has been our sufficiency through these days, and we do rejoice that we can trust His heart where we cannot trace His hand."

Herb and Jessie didn't look back. Herb's primary job was no less fascinating than Jessie's nursing. He, along with a young pastor who had just graduated from Bible school, had spiritual responsibility for 220 villages surrounding Sourou. Herb's goal was to establish a church in each of those 220 villages! "Church" was defined as a group of people meeting together to worship the God of the Bible. They would usually meet first under a thatched roof supported by rough poles. Then later, as the group grew in numbers and passion, volunteers would make mud bricks and erect a simple structure to protect themselves from sun, wind and rain.

Herb did a lot of traveling as he cared for his scattered flock. Often the family went along on these trips which sometimes had more adventure than anyone wanted—like the day the truck broke down, leaving them stranded by the side of the road. While they waited for help to arrive, the slow-flying gnats began to creep up their noses and into their ears and eyes. The only solution was to build a fire on that terribly hot and dusty day and stand in the smoke. Eventually they were rescued by a passing truck. Jessie and the children squeezed into the cab, leaving Herb, along with many Africans, perched on the back and hanging on for dear life. They made it back home, and many days later Herb was able to get his truck fixed and driven home.

Often on a Friday Herb would pack a suitcase and chop box. This chop box was basic to the survival of every early missionary. It contained a little camp stove, a cooking pot and usually bread and canned cheese, meat or tuna, along with coffee or tea. The idea was that by carrying a chop box, a missionary could ensure a healthy diet while traveling in areas where hygienic ways of preparing food weren't yet common practice. Women who cooked didn't always know the importance of cleanliness, and water sources were often contaminated.

But Herb soon tired of the chop box idea, and Jessie soon tired of seeing the chop box return just as she had packed it. She was more than happy to scratch the chop box off her Friday "to-do" list. As for Herb, he preferred to eat with his African friends, and he learned to love the dishes they prepared. The only luxuries Herb couldn't give up were salt, filtered drinking water (a necessity for good health; he'd carry a week's supply if necessary) and some hard candy to suck after a hot and spicy African meal.

Every Friday, he'd head off to one of his villages and settle under a spreading mango tree on a homemade wooden chair offered by friendly and often curious villagers. *Just why,* they wondered, *has this tall and smiling foreigner with the warm eyes come to our village?* And then the long exchange of greetings required in that culture would begin:

Chief: *I danse.* (Welcome.)
Herb: *Nba.* (Thanks.)
Chief: *Here be?* (Is there peace?)
Herb: *Here Doron.* (Only peace.)
Chief: *Bo yoro mogow don?* (How are your people?)
Herb: *U ka kene.* (They are well.)
Chief: *Sigi yoro be yen.* (There is a seat.)
Herb: *I ni ce.* (Thanks.)
Chief: *I ma ji min wa?* (Do you want to drink water?)
Herb: *Ji ko ka nyi.* (I don't need water.)
Chief: *Do di?* (What's the news?)

Herb: *Juguma te, foli don.* (Nothing serious, it is a greeting.)
Chief: *I ni ce foli la.* (Thank you for your greeting.)
Herb: *Ala k'an deme.* (May God help us.)
Chief: *Amina, Ala here ke an ye.* (Amen, may God give us peace.)
Herb: *Amina.* (Amen.)
Chief: *I ni ce foli la.* (Thank you for the greeting.)

And on it would go until Herb would have satisfied local courtesies and received permission to teach and preach about the "Jesus Road." If there were believers in the town, he'd spend extra time with them. In view of the shortage of pastors and church leaders in the area when Herb moved there, his goal was to work with local believers so some would eventually become spiritual leaders. After a day or two of teaching, evangelizing and encouraging, Herb would pack up and go on to the next village or return home until his next trip.

Herb and Jessie were particularly interested in the youth. They wanted to see more of them take Bible school training to become pastors and church leaders. Often, though, prospective students had limited Bible knowledge. Coupled with little or no formal schooling, this was a huge handicap. To address these problems, Jessie offered a three-week short-term Bible school course to prepare them for entry into the regular Bible school. With the help of a local teacher, she'd push and prod students through instruction in basic reading and writing as well as a dose of general Bible knowledge. At the end of the Nehlsens' first year at Sourou, six young men headed off to the Ntorosso Bible School in Mali.

Herb's mechanical abilities stood him in good stead, especially during his first term when there were few local mechanics. They were often a source of comfort to his fellow missionaries. He directed and did most of the work when a colleague's 1950 Studebaker three-quarter-ton pickup needed a ring job. In the process of tearing down the motor, he broke a stud bolt and then had to make a sixty-mile trip to the capital to find a bolt that would replace the broken one. The trip was successful, but a lot of time was lost.

In conformity with Mission policy, Jessie and Herb sent their firstborn, Becky, to the boarding school to begin first grade. The school was situated more than 800 miles away in Guinea. Getting there meant a three- or four-day trip over roads ranging from poor to impassable. Send a child away that far, that young? Even more than forty years later, raw grief is evident as Jessie continues to mourn Becky's first year at boarding school. "The single biggest mistake of our missionary career was to send Becky to school that year instead of waiting another year," she says, the pain still visible on her finely sculpted face.

From the day Becky left for boarding school, the Nehlsen's calendar was irrevocably changed. From then on, with submissive yet aching hearts, they counted the weeks, the days, until her return or until they could make the long trip to visit her. Sometimes that pilgrimage not only had the ultimate carrot at the other end, but it also meant a chance to take a much-needed break at a rest station near Dalaba, high in Guinea's mountains. There, where the climate was cooler, they were far from their dusty work environment, and they could happily relax while their children explored the fascinating terrain around them. Other missionary families would often be there too, so there was a lot of socializing. For Herb and Jessie, who often were isolated from others of their own language and culture, it was a special time.

One trip to Guinea is indelibly stamped in their memories. It was March, Becky's four-month vacation was coming to an end and days had to be spent in preparation for her return to school. First Jessie had to dig into their forty-five gallon storage drums to find the right size clothes and shoes for her growing daughter. Each item had to be carefully labeled with Becky's name as required by the school: each garment, sock, toothbrush, comb, etc.

The task of packing for the trip was enormous. There were literally mounds of equipment and food which had to be loaded into their International Travelall—things like basic tools in case of car trouble, enough drinking water for the entire three-day trip, bedding, towels and kitchen linens for the cottage, Becky's things, and then the food. The food—food for nearly three weeks! Food to eat during the travel days (each night of the trip they were received by missionary friends or stayed in Mission-run guest houses), but also food for their entire vacation.

There were no fast foods or mixes in those days; Jessie made everything from scratch. So there were tins of sugar, flour, oatmeal, margarine, coffee, tea, milk powder—everything Jessie needed to produce delicious meals for her family and the "others" who would inevitably gather around her table during the course of their vacation. Jessie never forgot her "secret of success"—her Betty Crocker cookbook. She knew she'd find basic dishes and pots and pans in the cottage but, being an exceptional cook, she always included a favorite knife or two along with Herb's favorite coffeepot.

Finally, all the preparations were complete, and Becky, as well as a very excited five-year-old Debbie, climbed into the truck with little Steve at their heels. They were off! How they all looked forward to those vacation days with their friends. Excited, the family took for granted the endless potholes, the dusty wind in their faces and the roadside "facilities," a sheltering bush.

But several things would take place before school began. The Alliance missionaries of West Africa would assemble for their annual conference in Kankan, Guinea. This was a refreshing time of fellowship as well as necessary business. Then many would drive to Dalaba where they would enjoy a much-needed break in the Mission-owned cluster of cottages.

Now, with conference over, they had one long day to Dalaba and fun vacation days. Doloris Burns Bandy explains what happened next.

> A caravan of missionary vehicles was snaking its way over the hilly dirty roads that led to Dalaba, the vacation mecca. Between Kankan, the Mission headquarters, and Mamou were two major rivers to be crossed by poled ferry.

This meant a very early start to get to the river. Even so we often waited several hours depending on truck traffic. Some families had left the night before and camped at the river in order to be first in line for the ferry.

The ferry was propelled by several Africans using long bamboo poles to navigate the swift currents in the channels. At the other side the ferrymen jumped off, tied ropes to tree stumps and lowered planks for disembarkment. Drivers then shifted into low gear and crept their vehicles slowly and carefully down onto the planks and to dry ground.

On this crossing there were four families aboard—the Nehlsens, Burnses, Adamses and Tylers. As Herb started off, his back wheels hung on the ferry as it drifted backward. We were behind them in the second car, watching as the water rose higher and higher. Inside was a family of five including baby Steve. I envisioned the ferry being swept downstream in the current to who-knows-where.

Tom pulled our car forward, as did those behind us, to put as much weight as possible on the front end of the ferry. At the very end of the ramp the front bumper of the Nehlsens' truck caught and held on some rough stones. Water was up to the car windows. Herb stepped out into waist-deep water. The ferrymen quickly brought a dugout canoe and one by one the family climbed out and into the canoe.

Our son, Stan, and David Adams were out of the trucks and into the water. They ran up the hill and found an abandoned tractor. The tractor, however, required a six-volt battery, and all our trucks used twelve-volt batteries. In God's provision, the McKinneys were waiting on the other side of the river. Mac's truck used a six-volt battery. Tom and Fordy Tyler went by dugout across the river and returned with the battery.

It worked. After a second try, the Nehlsen truck was slowly nudged from the runway and up the embankment. The dirty brown water had seeped into the trunk containing Becky's clothes, the vacation food, the linens and the tools. For years to come, the water-wrinkled pages of Jessie's salvaged cookbook showed stains where the river had invaded.

The risk of losing the vehicle, to say nothing of the lives at risk, the mind-boggling puzzle of how to retrieve the heavy truck, the ruined food and supplies, the long delay, the discomfort of waiting with three active children—it was a day to be endured and then filed away in memory's folder. But even this experience evoked a positive response, "Praise the Lord for His protection and watchful care in what could have been a fatal accident," wrote Jessie in a letter to friends and family.

By July of 1960, Becky was home from boarding school, the Nehlsens' first four-year term was completed and with great excitement the family of five headed back to Illinois for what was then called furlough (now home assignment). The highlight of that year would be the birth of Judith Ann, just forty-two minutes after Debbie's seventh birthday. Judi's birth, along with Herb's two tours, Jessie's many speaking engagements, countless hours of shopping, wonderful reunions with family and friends and the daily dramas of family life all added up to a memorable year. Refreshed and renewed and now numbering six, the Nehlsen family headed back to Africa for their second term aboard a freighter sailing out of New Orleans, Louisiana.

7

A Sacrifice of Limes

By the time Herb and Jessie were back on African soil after their first furlough, Upper Volta had gained its independence from France. The national church too had become independent from the Mission. The Nehlsens longed for the day when it would also be completely self-propagating, reaching out to every village in the district. At the time this seemed like an impossible dream in the region due to a division between the northern and southern Samo churches.

The problem started when two pastors from the southern Samo tribe married two girls from the northern Samo tribe. Some of the northern elders objected to the marriages, and a large and painful rift developed in the church. "It really boiled down to a form of racism," Jessie explained sadly. She and Herb worked to overcome this hurdle, praying and counseling. How they longed to see strong and vibrant churches in that region! They set aside a special day of prayer to plead with God for His resolution of the problem. A breakthrough came.

"God met us on that day, and the church has not been the same since. There were confessions of sin that could never be made except for the power of God through the Holy Spirit. There was restitution, asking forgiveness one of the other and of unsaved relatives and friends as well. Revival has come," the Nehlsens wrote home to friends.

God's power was evident in 1962 as well when the rains stopped too soon. For a people completely dependent on their fields for food, a lack of rain could easily mean terrible suffering and even death from starvation. The fetishers sacrificed goats and chickens for twenty days. Nothing happened. The Muslims prayed and sacrificed sheep for seven days. Nothing happened. The only thing left was to ask the small group of Christians in Sourou to pray. At 2 o'clock one afternoon, they met for prayer. At 6, the sky grew dark, but the wind came and blew the clouds away. The villagers began to say it looked like the Christians couldn't make it rain either. But the believers remained all night in fasting and prayer. At 9 o'clock the next morning the sky grew dark, and about 10 it started to rain. It rained and rained until even the hard heart of the local pastor's father melted, and he invited Jesus into his life.

And then sickness struck. First Herb became desperately ill. What could it be? There wasn't a reliable doctor or laboratory nearby. Then Becky and Debbie began to complain. Jessie knew they couldn't leave in a few days with the other children going to

Guinea to the MK (Missionary Kid) school. Then
Herb turned yellow, and they knew that the family
must have hepatitis.

Jessie prepared for the trip to their headquarters.
Herb drove to the next Mission station thirty miles
away, and their missionary colleague drove the remaining 110 miles to Bobo Dioulasso. The doctor
ordered a month's rest, flat in bed. One day, Jessie
told some concerned African women that their "big
father" really needed some limes; the juice would be
good for him. The women knew it wasn't the season
for citrus fruit, but they also knew that sometimes, in
a certain spot many miles away, limes could be
found. They made the long walk, found the coveted
fruit and brought it back to their beloved missionary.

Telling this story later, Herb's eyes filled with tears
and emotion choked his words. Pictures come to mind
of King David receiving water from Bethlehem's well
delivered at such great risk by his loyal men. David
couldn't even drink such precious water, so he poured
it out on the ground as an infinitely precious sacrifice
to Almighty God. Herb, on the other hand, chose to
drink the costly lime juice and then for years to come
he poured out his very life on a daily basis as a sacrifice
to God for the Samogo people.

A huge change was afoot! After much prayer and
discussion with Mission and church leaders, it was
decided that the Nehlsens would move from Sourou
to the larger town of Tougan. The Mission viewed
Tougan, the government center, as being the geo-
graphic and strategic center of the region. In fact,

the entire region was called "the Tougan region" after this important town.

Herb and Jessie were excited about the move.
From the more central location of Tougan it would
be easier for them and for church leaders to evangelize and disciple all parts of this large region. Several
of the Christians, however, said it would never work.
How could the regional headquarters for a Christian
church succeed in a town that was more than ninety
percent Muslim? Church work would never move
ahead in such a difficult context.

Convinced of the Lord's leading, the Nehlsens
moved anyway. Tougan, although an important com-
mercial center, in reality was just a dusty little place
with well under 10,000 inhabitants. When Herb and
Jessie arrived, there was not a single Protestant church
in the entire town—just mosques where Muslims
prayed. Undaunted, Herb and Jessie started to work
with what they had—praying friends in North America, the Holy Spirit, the Scriptures in the Bambara language, a young pastor just out of Bible school and a
handful of local believers.

The first sanctuary, built just after they arrived in
1962, was nothing more than a rough shelter made
of cornstalks. But it housed the Body of Christ, and
every month new believers came to faith. Herb
would ease his bulk onto a plank bench suspended
between stacks of mud-dried bricks and dream of
the day a solid chapel would replace the cornstalks.

The Nehlsens rented a house in town and then
started looking for property to purchase. A farmer
on the edge of town was willing to sell a parcel of

land and Herb's task began. He knew it couldn't all be finished before furlough was due the next year, but he would begin. With vivid memories of losing half of the roof on his previous house, he determined first to plant trees, lots of trees, a double row of fast-growing trees to encircle the yard as protection from the strong winds and to give necessary shade.

With the allotted $4,000, it was necessary to plan wisely. The big man—with the happy heart, the strong back, the childlike faith, the smart and supportive wife and a limitless supply of energy—started to work. First a well had to be dug. Next, Herb, who had never built a house, counseled with others concerning a plan: how many pressed mud/cement bricks would be needed and where could he find a good local mason? They worked together, building the garage and outbuilding (an office, storeroom and outside kitchen unit).

Weekends Herb spent "in the bush," evangelizing and meeting with little groups of believers. Occasionally the whole family would spend a week in one of the villages, living in their little trailer and having classes all day with a service at night. This they called "short-term Bible school" and was a highlight for the believers in those villages.

The last big project was laying the foundation for their future home. But then things had to come to a standstill. It was the summer of 1965 and time for furlough.

Their second term had been both blessed and difficult. The work in the Tougan district had advanced through the two human instruments God had in His providence placed there. It was accompanied by on-going family dramas like when Jessie tragically lost another baby, Steven went off to school and Becky and Debbie moved from the boarding school in Guinea to one in neighboring Ivory Coast, 500 miles nearer home.

Hurriedly their earthly possessions were moved into the completed garage and outbuilding unit. Farewells were said—"until next year." It was not easy leaving this infant church but they knew God's Spirit remained with them. It would have been even harder if they had known just how long it would be before they returned.

Herb and Jessie, along with Becky, thirteen; Debbie, twelve; Steve, seven; and Judi, four, headed back to the United States, eager for the next Illinois chapter in their lives.

Once again they were given the Wheaton home of Jessie's parents to be their furlough home. They were enjoying times with family, friends and supporting churches, not knowing that a surprise awaited them. Several months into their furlough, a request came from headquarters asking them to be houseparents at Ivory Coast Academy (ICA) in Bouaké (BWA-kay), Ivory Coast for two years. That meant being "dad" and "mom" to twenty-nine MKs (missionary kids). The decision was not easy. What about Tougan, the unreached villages, the unfinished house? But, they knew that MKs too are important and they willingly said "Yes" to this important assignment.

Then the request came, "Would you please bring out a long list of furnishings needed for this new dormitory?" All sorts of supplies and furnishings were needed to get the dorm fully functional. Getting all this organized was just the sort of job to bring special joy to the heart of Wholesale Herb!

The list of items was long and included a very special one, a piano. Herb and Jessie's hearts were in this project. They could just picture scores of missionary children in years to come taking turns to play a tune, practice scales and then proudly perform for visiting parents. A piano, though, would be costly to buy. The Nehlsens knew they'd need the help of some "giving specialists," people who had enough zeal and experience to tackle such a project.

So they went to the district president of the Alliance Women (then called Women's Missionary Prayer Fellowship), and together they formulated a plan to have willing women collect S&H green stamps offered by certain retailers. Once a booklet of 100 stamps was collected, for example, it could be redeemed toward the purchase of a wide range of items, a piano among them. The pile of booklets slowly started to grow. Herb and Jessie watched with amazement and delight as they continued to arrive. They knew that each book of stamps represented great generosity. Women could easily have used those stamps to buy things for themselves, but instead, they chose to buy a piano for the children of their missionaries.

The big day finally arrived. Herb took all the booklets to a designated office, traded the stamps for a voucher, and then took the voucher to a piano store. There a Christian dealer gave him an exceptional deal on a piano still in the crate in which it had arrived from Japan. This two-pronged bargain—the affordable price and already having the piano crated—set the tone as the Nehlsens ordered a large container from the Illinois Central Railway. They were given a twenty-four-hour deadline to pack the container before a truck would arrive to pick it up. Such a feat would be possible only with church friends pitching in and working nearly around the clock.

All the donations Herb and Jessie had received during their furlough year were carefully loaded into that container: two washers, two dryers, every kind of kitchen equipment you can imagine, the green-stamps piano, furnishings for the dorm parents' apartment, linens, pots and pans and even some furniture. And all the Tougan supplies were tucked in too—a windmill, tools, spare parts, canned food, clothing and medicine. The carefully packed container followed the rails to the dock and was eventually loaded onto a freighter heading to Abidjan. Jessie and the children would fly back to Africa, but Herb and his friend Clyde Ritchie would travel by sea, accompanying the precious container.

8

The Old Rugged Cross/
The Black Metal Cross

While they were still on the high seas, arrangements were being made in Africa to receive the container. Côte d'Ivoire field chairman, Joe Ost, another wheeler/dealer of sorts, was working on the necessary paperwork and searching for the largest semitrailer truck he could find. In his opinion, the truck he finally rented was the biggest to be found anywhere in the entire country. It was ready and waiting at the dock the day the ship started unloading. Herb and Clyde had already disembarked. How excited they were as they watched the container's contents being transferred to the giant truck!

When the truck seemed ready to roll, one significant problem became alarmingly evident—the truck's battery was dead. The only way to get the semi started without impossible delays was to push it. But the only direction to push it was down the quay toward the Atlantic Ocean! A group of men got behind each big set of wheels and started to push. Herb put his own large shoulder behind a wheel knowing that after the truck started, if it couldn't stop in time, his entire container would end up deep in the bay! He pushed, he prayed. The truck rolled, jerked, paused for a heartbeat, and . . . the engine caught. The driver hit the brakes, and the giant vehicle came to a stop just short of the tepid waters of the dockside drink.

Even that oversized truck couldn't hold all the provisions Herb and Jessie had collected during their furlough year. Joe Ost's pickup was also packed to capacity and still more had to be left behind until Herb could make another trip to pick it all up. Wholesale Herb had outdone himself!

With the furnishings for the dorm finally delivered and in place, the Nehlsens began the search for a reliable car. Their first find was a Ford Taurus van. When its motor burned out, they put in a Peugeot motor and changed it to a stick shift. Even Herb had to admit that it never worked very well. The family once drove the van on a holiday to Ghana with colleague Kay Thompson. The tales of that trip were later stored away in their memory bank under the title, "The Car We Pushed Around Ghana with Kay."

Herb and Jessie thoroughly enjoyed their life at ICA, being near their own children as well as taking part in all the extracurricular activities, plays, parties, recitals and sports events. They looked forward to snack time at night when their family of twenty-nine would gather for treats and fun before devotions and nighttime hugs. Herb liked sneaking out with the boys on Saturday morning with their BB guns to see if they could bring home some rabbits or field mice.

But as the second year began, they felt more and more the tug to return to their ministry in Upper Volta. Jerry and Nora McGarvey, missionaries in Mali, graciously offered to come for the second semester and relieve them of their responsibilities.

So in January 1968, with great joy, they traveled north to Tougan, the place that was now "home." On arrival they rejoiced to see that nothing had stood still in their absence. The churches in the region had grown in both numbers and maturity. The Nehlsens had to ask God's forgiveness for their lack of faith. They had not needed to fear that their long absence would be a hindrance to the advance of the church in that area.

Herb knew that his first task would be the building of their home, while the family "camped" in the outbuilding and a small trailer. Herb, together with an excellent African mason, built a solid cement block, three-bedroom, one-bathroom home. With cement floors and plastered and painted walls, it was simple but very adequate. Longtime pastor friends Paul and Melba Stumbo from Minnesota came for several months to give invaluable help, installing ceilings and cabinets. Other missionary colleagues used their abilities to assist with other tasks.

Since the $4,000 couldn't stretch any further, Herb and Jessie had to dip into their personal funds to build their "favorite room," a long screened veranda off of the dining room and master bedroom. That was the main spot for all family meals, but it also became their favorite spot to sleep during the hot months when sleeping inside became unbearable.

By February 1969 they were ready, more than ready, to move into what they considered their "spacious" new home, though in the U.S. it would have been considered very modest.

One day, a cynical young man from North America was visiting Herb. "How can you, a missionary, justify having the nicest house for miles around?" he asked with obvious disapproval.

Herb was silent a moment, then turned to an African pastor by his side.

"What do you think about that question?" he asked.

The pastor didn't hesitate. Looking directly at Herb, he responded.

"If this was your house, maybe we'd mind. But it isn't just yours, its ours too. We're at home when we're here."

Outside the kitchen door, Herb built a sort of breezeway connecting his office, storeroom and outside kitchen to the main house. It was in this breezeway that Jessie set up what she called her "backdoor dispensary." The move to Tougan had signaled a major change for Jessie's medical work. At Sourou she had worked in a government-built dispensary with office hours and more-or-less established routines. The move to Tougan took her medical practice out of an institution and into her home. As people became familiar with the location and the TLC that was dispensed there, more and more people found their way to her door. It was not unusual for eighty or more patients to find their way to her back door each morning. Her dispensary enjoyed official favor as a designated clinic for that part of town.

At first she had one cupboard for her medicines; then she added a second and a third. Herb could have built her a separate dispensary, but she liked the convenience of working out of her home and being able to close the door whenever it was necessary to get away. On Thursdays, for example, she closed her dispensary so she could teach at a nearby girls' school. Today, years after her departure from Tougan, the local dispensary which replaced hers still closes on Thursdays. The spirit of Jessie still hovers there.

Some of Jessie's medical cases were routine—ears cleaned with peroxide, prescriptions filled from her medicine cupboard, etc. But others took longer, such as a burned hand needing each finger wrapped separately or an hour-long treatment for tapeworms.

As patients waited their turn to see Jessie, she would sometimes play gospel recordings. She was never completely comfortable, though, with a teaching method which people could choose to ignore if they wanted to visit with each other. Jessie would try to be sensitive to what the Holy Spirit was telling her. When she sensed His nudging, she'd lay down her syringe, pick up her flashcards and tell her captive audience of God's love for each one of them. They heard not only her words, but they also saw her hands dispensing His healing love day after day.

One sweltering day, things weren't going well in Jessie's breezeway dispensary. Patients seemed irritable and slow to grasp what she was telling them. Interruptions were many. Finally, even calm and dignified

Jessie lost her cool. Later, alone in her room, remembering that Samos view temper displays as being very serious—right up there with adultery—Jessie was filled with remorse. Her remorse turned to grief when she picked up a *World Vision* magazine and saw a picture of a needy child under the caption, "If they don't see Jesus in you, they'll never see Jesus at all." As Jessie asked the Lord to forgive her, she ripped the picture from the magazine and, hurrying to her dispensary, taped that poignant sentiment to the outside of the medicine cupboard door so she would never forget it.

But it wasn't always easy to stay calm and be Christlike. African children were often afraid of this pale foreigner, and mothers would prey on these fears by saying in essence, "Be good, or I'll give you to the white woman, and she'll eat you!" After threats like that, was it any wonder the children would scream in terror when Jessie went to examine them? With sweat running down her face and another forty patients waiting to be seen, times like that tested Jessie's resolve and threw her onto the Lord for His patience, His peace, His priorities.

Herb found himself facing a new challenge, one well suited to this friendly man with a burden for lost people. The Mission leaders asked him to help implement a program called New Life For All (NLFA), a method of evangelism and discipleship that had been born in Africa and was very user-friendly in the context of Africa's oral tradition. To illustrate truth, it used graphics rather than words which few would have been able to read. Herb, along with Bob Pease, a missionary from Mali, would travel from church district to church district showing pastors and leaders how to implement the program in their area. Each of those visits took about a week. And so, from April to September of 1969 Herb traveled in the district, leaving Jessie with her many responsibilities.

The Christians were taught to gather in prayer cells for daily prayer focused exclusively on their unconverted friends and relatives. Herb spent the first sessions explaining who was qualified to pass on this training to others. The first requirement was that they had to be believers themselves. This was Herb's chance to ensure that all church leaders were solidly converted. Nothing was taken for granted. During the next five sessions, Herb would show church leaders how to teach their own people to evangelize in this way. There was also an apprenticeship component in which Herb would accompany church leaders around the village or town as they shared their faith one-on-one using a small tract containing images only, no words. Hundreds were saved during these forays.

But it was hard work—very hard work. Camping in the bush was no picnic. There were hot, hot days, uncomfortable sleeping arrangements, strange foods, no plumbing and never a glass of ice water. But the blessings were innumerable as Herb saw people saved and believers strengthened. One added blessing for Herb was having his son Steve, who had just finished fifth grade, travel with him for several weeks. In fact, when Steve was growing up, during every school vacation he'd be out in the villages many weekends with his father. From the time the boy was in sixth grade, Herb would often ask him to say a few words whenever there was a service. Steve would testify to his faith in Jesus Christ. But that wasn't all—those times were a lot of fun too.

The ritual was predictable. Herb would pack up the car, finally inserting the cots which would be their beds, and then Jessie would come out with a batch of sweet rolls for them to take along. One day, Herb decided to take their little "Diane," a tiny French car he had purchased for Jessie to use during his frequent absences. Steve said the car was so small that it always felt as though they were going around a corner due to Herb's significant poundage lowering one side and Steve's boyish frame unable to balance it on the other! On that particular trip, they were headed to a village thirty miles off the main road. Before they had gone far, a heavy rain nearly stopped them in their tracks. But far from getting stuck in the wet sand and mud, the miniature car acted like a skateboard sailing gracefully around the edges of the deep water holes.

The problem was that darkness was descending sooner than usual, thanks to the ominous storm clouds. Herb was having trouble seeing the road. He sent Steve ahead by foot, but soon got out of the car himself to investigate. The mud was incredibly slippery. There was big Herb, sliding around on the mud and landing on his back more than once. They couldn't help it. Both Herb and Steve convulsed with laughter. That day's storm provided a wonderful memory which neither of them tired of retelling.

Arrival at the village didn't spell an end to the memory-making moments. Steve remembers setting up the cots under a tree and awaking to find donkeys

and chickens walking around his bed, keeping a
close watch on this young white boy. Herb always
liked to bring a flashlight to the evening meal so he
could see what was in the sauce he was served. However, one night he forgot his flashlight. A few bites
into the meal, he confided in Steve that the crunchy
morsel he had bitten into was actually the head of a
chicken! Steve offered his sympathy. The reply was
typically Herb: "Oh, well. You can't see it, so that's
half the battle." And big Herb kept right on chewing.

As Steve got older, Herb gave him more responsibility until, during his high school years, Steve prepared
and delivered brief sermons. Herb would often ask his
opinion too about things they encountered along the
way.

Meanwhile, back in Tougan, Jessie saw her medical work mushroom in spite of the complication of
the many languages spoken in the area. Since she
understood only Jula and French, she decided to
hire a woman to help treat patients and to translate
when necessary. Teresa, the middle-aged wife of a
Muslim man, was a faithful Christian who was tuned
in to the voice of the Holy Spirit.

One day, as Jessie and Teresa were treating one patient after another, Teresa turned to Jessie and said,
"We should stop right now and share about Jesus."
Jessie followed her advice and proceeded to tell her patients about the sacrifice Jesus had made for them.
One of them, a woman, asked a few questions. Before
the morning was over, Jessie and Teresa had led her to
a saving knowledge of Jesus Christ.

The African grapevine was soon buzzing about the good care patients received at the Protestant Mission. Malaria, dysentery, diarrhea, tetanus, burns, sores and every sort of parasite—all were treated with tender care. And when the annual cool season arrived, there would be the inevitable pneumonia, measles and meningitis epidemics. With no laboratory or X ray, God Himself became Jessie's wisdom, guide and ever-present companion.

Even as Jessie was exercising her spiritual gift of mercy on the back porch, God was continuing to build His Church in the Tougan region.

Another ministry was opening for Herb. Two of his spiritual gifts—evangelism and helps—had formed a wonderful marriage in a colportage ministry. By buying stocks of Bibles and Christian books in the capital city and then sending them out with pastors to sell in the Tougan area, he was able to get the Word of God to many people. As pastors sold the books and counseled their customers, they'd also earn a bit of extra money to feed their families. Evangelizing while earning money? Herb's big heart resonated with that combination!

Pastor François was one of the pastors Herb helped to set up as a colporteur. But a thief was eating up the pastor's small profits. When the culprit was finally caught, grief turned to anger. It was the pastor's own son, Matthew. Herb and Jessie decided to pray especially for the boy. Finally, the Lord started to answer those prayers. Matthew turned back to the Lord and left his thieving ways behind. Herb taught him to drive, and Matthew showed his complete change of heart by going back to school as an adult. Today, Matthew is a chauffeur and a pillar in the Tougan church. A musically gifted young man, he started writing hymns in his own language. And when Herb and Jessie left Africa for the last time, he presented them with a beautifully hand-carved musical instrument made of true ebony, jet black with swirls of blond. Matthew explained, "This is to show that black people and white people can make beautiful music together."

Herb's colportage ministry not only helped his pastor friends earn some money, but also when youth groups from North America came to spend the summer in ministry, Herb encouraged them to sell Bibles as a method of village evangelism. They'd fan out, two by two, with a local interpreter, to sell their books, Bibles and school supplies. People would come around to see their wares, and the youth would then invite everyone to an open-air meeting later that evening.

Sometimes they showed films at night. Jessie's father, James Wilson Ewing, II, passed away, and her family wanted to choose a memorial project that would help the Nehlsens' ministry. They decided to purchase two Moody Science films. These films powerfully portrayed the fact that the God of creation (a fact which Muslims did not question) was the God of the Bible, and His Son Jesus was not just a prophet but the Savior of the world.

In Tougan itself, where not a single Protestant church had existed before the arrival of Herb and Jessie, the Nehlsens along with two young men started to hold services. Slowly, slowly, others began to come until a core group of thirty-five adults was meeting under the cornstalk shelter. They were all dirt poor. Most had neither financial resources nor formal schooling, but they were growing babes in Christ. The need for a church building was heavy on Herb and Jessie's hearts. The cornstalk shelter was already too small. So the Nehlsens, their family and American and local friends began to ask the Lord for a lot in the center of town and for money to build a simple church. A lot and some money. Was that too hard for God?

The answer to those prayers appeared when a Lebanese man, a local Muslim merchant, offered to sell them a large property close to the central market. Now they could start building! The people didn't have money to contribute, but they could work. Herb could raise money from family and faithful friends in the United States—and he also had buckets of sweat and countless ideas to offer. His was a rather unique way of approaching a project. He'd come up with an idea and then enthusiastically move toward making that idea a reality even though at the beginning he really wouldn't have any idea how he was going to accomplish it. But he'd start with a vision, and then treat it like a big, exciting puzzle. How was he going to get from A to Z? He just knew there was a way, and he was going to find it.

Field chairman and experienced builder Tom Burns designed the roof and Herb, in his own yard, using equipment from his well-stocked shop, welded together the metal girders according to Tom's design. Thankfully, Wholesale Herb had the tools he needed to do the job; almost nothing was available locally.

Once the welding project was complete, the church people, men and women, started trickling into the missionary's yard where they lifted those heavy girders up onto their thin shoulders and walked out the gate and down the main street of that Muslim town. Arriving at the new church property, they laid their burdens down. They probably weren't aware of the symbolic prophecy they were making—many heavy spiritual burdens would later be laid down in that very place.

When Herb did something, he did it well. This church had to be as attractive as he could make it. Fresh in his mind were the granite-faced flower boxes running the length of his own newly constructed house. That type of granite would go a long way to enhancing the front of the new chapel and making it look like a building of importance. So Herb hired a trucker to go into the country and bring back a load of big granite stones.

Then, working with Tom Burns, Herb supervised as a local builder carefully cemented those granite rocks into two columns on the chapel's front face, leaving space for a cross in between. Sometimes the rocks were too big, but after some sledge hammer assaults, pieces of the large stones were carefully cemented in place. When the columns were finally finished, the only thing lacking was a cross.

So, undaunted, Herb went in pursuit of material to construct a cross. He found a junk dealer ready to sell him almost a ton of scrap steel—old girders. Working in his own yard, Herb welded the girders into the shape of a cross, had it sanded and then finished it by

In November, 1951, after a five-year romance, Herb and I tied the knot in our home church in Villa Park, Illinois.

God's leading into nursing came as a surprise to me, but His plan became clear once I stepped on African soil.

Herb's father was very proud of him when he decided to serve Uncle Sam, but he opposed his serving God.

Our pre-missionary pastoral experience was in a small country church in Lorimor, Iowa. Our first daughter, Becky, was born in 1952 at the hospital where I trained.

Becky was almost three and Debbie a year and a half when we received our assignment to Upper Volta, West Africa (now called Burkina Faso).

"To the Regions Beyond" is the song that went through our minds as we drove three days to our new home in Sourou.

We hadn't been in Africa long when a wind storm tore the sheet metal off one side of our roof, allowing the rain to pour down the mud walls.

This was a memorable example of the importance of "holding the ropes" in prayer for missionaries. When these men didn't hold the ropes, our vehicle fell off into the river, and the ferry began dragging us back out into the current.

African desert seasons are hot and hotter. Even the big candles (bottom left) had trouble standing straight.

I was always uncomfortable when Herb was on top of the windmill. But we were certainly grateful for the tasty fruit we enjoyed because of the water it produced. A kind farmer in the U.S. gave us the windmill.

This is one of the reasons we carried a flashlight at night. Not only could a python be on his way to steal our chickens, but scorpions or smaller, more deadly snakes might also be on the path.

Moving day, African style. Enlist your friends, and pile it high!

This lovely Starcraft camper, a gift from the Monticello (Minnesota) Alliance Church, made our weeks spent teaching in the villages so much easier. I called it my "Waldorf Astoria."

The two-and-a-half years we spent at Ivory Coast Academy (ICA) being Mom and Dad to twenty-nine MKs were a lot of work but even more fun.

Pastor Bassan was the only pastor in our district when we arrived on the field in 1956. Since he was familiar with the language and with the large area, he was a great encouragement to Herb.

This family photo was taken in 1966. Children, L to R, top: Debbie, Becky, Bottom: Steve and Judi.

Evangelism, our first priority, was sometimes one-on-one, but frequently in the open air at village marketplaces.

We believe that God's Word is quick and powerful to work in people's lives and change their hearts. It was always encouraging to see them surround our book table.

Rebecca, Pastor Francois' wife, was happiest when she was explaining the "Jesus road" that leads to heaven.

The first church in any village is a corn-stalk shelter (right). This first building in Tougan (above) was built in 1970. It was a big step of faith because at the time only about 35 people were meeting together.

Both contractor, Glen Manske, and Steve and his four friends from St. Paul Bible College dreamed of helping to build our "Miracle Church." It was hard, muscle-building work in temperatures that often reached 100 degrees in the shade. In the providence of God this manpower was also used to build much-needed dormitories at the Kassan school.

God "just happened" to have some Canadian government
road builders nearby while the church was under construction. They
offered to transport the iron beams from our yard to the church.
What backbreaking work that would have been without their assistance!

God filled the Miracle Church. It now has two services—one in French and
one in the national language. Two faithful pastors shepherd over 500 people.

The Alliance Youth Corps often shared in our ministry. We traveled
some terrible roads together, the van loaded with projector and screen,
suitcases, sleeping bags, food and sleeping gear.

In 1973, our ministry changed drastically when crop failures compelled us to engage in relief ministries. These women were able to carry home their entire crop on their heads instead of using donkey carts as was their custom.

God provided a famine relief coordinator for us when Adama, a Muslim and an educated retired soldier, was born again and delivered from demons.

These women (below) waited all day if necessary to have their basins, buckets or sacks filled with grain. This blind man (left) often came with his children. He was always so grateful for what we gave him.

Another ministry was providing wells. The wells in many villages were running dry. These women (right) wait for water to trickle into the well so they can fill their containers.

The pastors' wives retreat was always a highlight. Now, sometimes as many as 100 women attend. They share in the cooking and sleep on grass mats.

After Matomo heard about Jesus and asked Him into her life, she told us she was now able to sleep through the night, no longer troubled by demons.

Sometimes dozens of patients were already waiting at our gate when we opened the clinic at 7 a.m.

Herb gives one of his bear hugs to a graduating student at the Bible school. When we arrived in Tougan, there was only one pastor, Pastor Francois, pictured right. When we left Africa in 1999, there were over 80 pastors serving the Tougan district.

Pastor Francois and Rebecca were people of little money but great faith. They trusted God for a motorbike to be dedicated to their ministry. God granted their request.

How we looked forward to the weekly mail delivery to our local post office. "As cool water to a weary soul, so is good news from a far country." We are grateful to so many people who wrote us, and especially to Ned and Esther Haugan who faithfully sent out our prayer letters, thus keeping our needs before more that 1,000 people.

Just before we retired, we made a return trip "home" to Tougan.
It turned into a grand celebration as the people welcomed us into
the church with singing and waving of banners.

In 1992, our entire family gathered for a final Africa reunion
before our retiral. Two grandchildren have since been added.
L to R back row: Becky, Judi, Herb, Jessie, Larry, Debbie.
L to R front row: Steve and Amy, with Abby, Andrea and Nathan.

Herb and Jessie Nehlsen, 1991.

layering on some black paint. With church people, workers and missionaries alike puffing and panting, the cross was pulled up and into place against the front of the building. Herb welded it to a piece of metal left protruding from the wall for just that purpose. God had worked a miracle. There was now both a physical and spiritual church there in the Muslim town of Tougan.

Meanwhile, the leaders of the region came to Herb and asked how they should organize the church work of the area. After thought and prayer, Herb responded, "Well, I think you should form a committee of pastors, and every month this committee should meet. Every other month have a larger meeting with every pastor and lay pastor in attendance, with each one being accompanied by the head elder or an assistant from his church." This idea sat well with the African custom of always having a witness present for any important event or conversation.

But Herb wasn't finished.

"That's not all," he said. "When we meet together, let's first have a time of devotions. Someone will teach from the Word of God. Then we'll give testimonies of God's work among us and in the district. After that, let's share prayer requests, and then we'll pray together. Only after all of that will we begin to conduct any business we might have."

"I didn't know anything about organizing a group of churches in a region," Herb admits. "It was the Lord who led me to have prayer and worship first, because the Lord knew that, by the time Bible study, prayer and worship were over, business could then

be conducted easily in a harmonious atmosphere."
Other missionaries have mused that the growth and
spiritual strength of the Tougan district today can no
doubt be contributed in large measure to the ongoing teaching and training the leaders received in
those regional meetings. These meetings, prayerfully
proposed and conducted so many years ago, continue to the present.

Thus the churches in the Tougan area were organized and began to grow and mature. Pastors were
trained, new villages were reached and villagers were
taught about the Jesus Road. Evangelism, discipleship, basic literacy and Bible training plus advanced
training for pastors and leaders—all this was actively
promoted and executed by Herb and Jessie. There
were also conferences for pastors, conferences for
women and camps for youth. Herb and Jessie were
always right there making things happen, transport-
ing people, helping to organize the food and lodging
details and then preaching or teaching when invited.

Two days before the Nehlsens' third furlough,
Tougan's first evangelical church building—a solid,
little structure with a beautiful stone face and strik-
ing black cross—was publicly dedicated to the glory
of God. Hallelujah! When Herb and Jessie left, they
had not only left a church building with a growing
body of believers in the town of Tougan, but they
had also left a church region that was growing nu-
merically and maturing. Physically and emotionally
depleted, they started back to North America for a
year of renewal and reporting. On their way home,
they passed through Europe and did a little touring.

As Jessie marveled at the massive cathedrals with their priceless artwork, she thought back to the little granite-faced chapel in Tougan. It was modest, but it too had been built at enormous cost in terms of sweat, ingenuity, love, determination and prayer.

Both Herb and Jessie were big believers in the power of prayer. Because of that, they never stopped asking people to pray for the district of Tougan. Their letters home always contained very strong directives— they weren't suggesting people pray, they were telling people they must pray! The list of friends receiving those blunt appeals grew to over 1,100 names as the Nehlsens' missionary career continued. As Jessie put it, "When the battle raged, we would pray, 'Lord, please remind our partners to pray; the battle is too great for us.' "

Years later, an aging Herb told of meeting one of their faithful prayer partners. "One dear lady came who sent us to the field in 1955 and has prayed faithfully for us ever since. . . . She is ninety-four, sharp as can be and very alert, remembers all the names and things. I just sat and wept as this dear saint told of praying for us during all these years. If one picture is worth a thousand words, then one visit like that is worth twenty-five years of service to the King."

When Herb and Jessie set their faces toward furlough they weren't just anticipating family and friends and a good rest. They would also be seeking those God had called to partner with them in prayer—prayer for the Samogo of the Tougan area of Burkina Faso.

During that furlough year, history repeated itself. Once again an S.O.S. came from the field. "Will you be willing to return for one more year to be houseparents for those special MKs?" They thought they had "graduated" but their answer was, "Yes, we'll accept the challenge—with joy."

9

A Big-Car Mentality

The year at ICA was full of activity, work and ministry to young hearts. One missionary parent visiting her children questioned Herb, "You seem so happy here. Won't you return to Upper Volta?"

Herb's response was, "Certainly we'll come back, but God has placed us here for this year, so why not be happy?"

So in July 1972 they were once again heading north, this time pulling a Starcraft camper. "You've got people looking at you when you go to sleep and still watching when you wake up!" was how visitor, Paul Stumbo, described village life when Herb took him out teaching and preaching in the district. Friendly Herb really didn't mind the curious stares of villagers, but he and Jessie were delighted when the Stumbos decided to raise money for a new and improved camper for the Nehlsens' village ministry.

The Alliance church in Monticello, Minnesota, spurred on by Paul and Melba, really got into the project. They divided an imaginary camper into pieces and sold a

tire to one person, a trailer hitch to another and so on until enough money had been pledged to buy the entire
camper. Once in Africa, the camper made a first-class
bush motel for the Nehlsens and in between trips served
as a guest house. It even had an indoor bathroom!

It was bright spots like the camper which stood in con-
trast to some harder things that happened during Herb
and Jessie's fourth term. They had returned to Africa
with a strong sense that their work was not finished; the
Lord had much more for them to do there in the Tougan
area. This poem was included in the letter they sent to
friends on the eve of their departure for Africa:

Would You?

If you had been to heathen lands
   where weary souls stretch out their hands
      to plead, yet no one understands,
         would you go back?
           Would you?

If you had seen the women bear
   their heavy loads with none to share,
      had heard them weep with none to care,
         would you go back?
           Would you?

If you had seen them in despair
   and beat their breasts and pull their hair
      while demon powers filled the air,
         would you go back?
           Would you?

If you had seen the glorious sight
   when heathen people in their night
      were brought from darkness into light,

would you go back?
Would you?

Yet still they wait, a weary throng,
they've waited, some so very long;
when shall despair be turned to song?
We're going back!
Would you?

—Author unknown; quoted in the Nehlsen's newsletter, July, 1971

So back they went, but not without enormous personal sacrifice. Both Becky and Debbie stayed in the U.S. Becky, who had already been in the States for two years of high school, was now in college. And Debbie, thanks to the generosity of some friends, enrolled for her last year of high school at Ben Lippen, a Christian boarding school located in the beautiful mountains of North Carolina. (ICA went only to eleventh grade at that time.)

The next year she wrote from college, "Some of the kids here are homesick. They are just now learning what I learned last year, that Jesus can be your best friend." Comments like that and Debbie's overall happiness in the U.S. helped comfort Jessie and Herb, but, oh, how they missed those girls!

When they finally arrived back in Tougan that summer of 1972, tremendous blessing and terrible tragedy were both awaiting them. The blessing came in early September when God sent a powerful revival sweeping through Mali and Upper Volta in areas where The Christian and Missionary Alliance was working. Evangelist Neill Foster from Canada was God's instrument to touch missionaries and nationals alike at that time. Milt Pierce reported:

A pastors' conference for all of the Upper Volta pastors was scheduled in Dédougou. I left the chairman's office that day, and before departing thought that I had better take some money with me in case of need. Opening the Mission safe, I found only large bundles of 500 franc notes. I took a couple of these and stuffed them into a briefcase. It wasn't until the end of the week that I knew how the Lord had arranged all of this.

The meetings started off in Dédougou with an eager expectation of what was going to happen. Those who had experienced or heard of the events in Bobo were doubtless the most expectant. . . . Missionaries took the lead in humbling themselves before the Lord and confessing their lack of love. There was resistance on the part of some of the pastors present. . . .

At the end of the week, as I talked to Neill early one morning, he asked me if I had a good sum of money in small bills. He explained that the Lord had spoken to him as he read in First John 3:17: "If anyone has material possessions and sees his brother in need but has no pity on him, how can the love of God be in him?" Neill went on to say that he had money with him that, divided among the sixty-three pastors present, would amount to 500 francs for each one, and he wanted to give this as a special gift to the pastors. It was obviously no coincidence that the

Mission safe had contained only large bundles of 500-franc notes. Where would I have found sixty-three such bills in Dédougou otherwise?

After a slow beginning . . . Jerry [McGarvey] reports what happened. "The next morning was something else! After a message on how we are required to love one another if we are to call ourselves Christ's disciples, Mr. Foster asked that all bow their heads. He said, 'You can say that God loves you. You can say that you love God. But can you turn to the one sitting next to you and say you love him? Is there anyone in the room to whom you cannot truthfully say, 'I love you'?"

Jerry said, "It was just like before a violent rain storm when the sky is black, but in one hushed moment all you can hear is the faraway faint roar of the coming wind." He continued, "Then it happened! Everyone was out of his seat. We were no longer shaking hands; we were hugging each other. Forgiveness was asked, and love was expressed as we shared this moment of divine love together, passing from one to another in what must be called an explosion of love. . . ."

I described it as a virtual Pentecost, the nearest thing to Acts 2 that I could imagine. There were no incidents of speaking in tongues during the revival, but had they occurred and been in order, I doubt any would have objected. Obviously it was an experience never to be forgotten. . . .

The weeks and months following the departure of Neill Foster witnessed still greater things as the flame of revival spread from local church to local church. Etienne Sanou from the Santidougou district was one who seemed to have received a portion of the Spirit that was upon Neill Foster. His ministry was extremely blessed everywhere he went for months following. The district churches responded openly, and space doesn't allow to recount all that took place. It was not unusual to have people from the churches walk up to you and break down in tears confessing everything from a lack of love to having stolen a nail from your workshop, so tender were consciences during those days. There was no explanation possible for it other than a miracle of God's grace.

Neill also remembers those momentous days in Dédougou:

The explosion of love came at the end of the message on Observable Love. I said to my interpreter, Jerry McGarvey, "*Ne be i kanu*—I love you." Jerry responded with the same words. Suddenly, as if a match had been put to gasoline, the meeting erupted. Everyone was expressing love everywhere. There were rivers of tears and embraces everywhere. Herb was as mighty in his tears as he was in his exuberant hugs and expressions of love and joy. Was there anyone, black or white, who was not dissolved in tears? I think not.

I also remember Rosalys Tyler publicly confessing to the African pastors that she had not
loved them as she should. Pastor Levi, in
sandy-colored clothes that matched his ebony
skin and white hair, responded, "You are our
mother. You brought the gospel to us. We do
forgive you."

The blessing continued. When we arrived
back in Tougan, Herb and Jessie's station, the
pastor who had been at the retreat did a most
unusual thing—he rang the church bell on Saturday. The people gathered. What he said I do
not know, but I do remember that with many
tears he sang every verse of "Jesus Keep Me
Near the Cross"—all this among people of
whom it was said, "They never cry."

Herb and Jessie experienced this powerful moving
of God's Spirit during a time of drought in the Tougan
area. During their furlough absence, many wells had
gone dry, some for as long as five months. Fortunately,
Herb was able to dig their own well deeper and find
water, but the drought had caused the water level to
drop throughout the entire district. This created terrible hardships for an already poverty-stricken population. Women and children would walk miles to
another village only to return with a pitifully small
amount of water. They'd carry it in basins on their
heads, covering the water's surface with leaves to help
contain it. But even that precaution didn't stop some
of the precious liquid from splashing over the sides
during the long walk home.

People would come to Jessie and Herb to say that
every well in their village was dry and that they had to
walk to the next village for water. In many villages
women stayed up all night to draw the drops of mois-
ture that trickled slowly into the well. And what was
even worse was that in some villages, particularly the
predominantly Muslim villages, Christians were told
there wasn't enough water for them. In the face of so
much human suffering, Herb's gift of mercy and his
many practical skills wouldn't let him sit idly by.

Both World Relief and the Alliance gave money to
help in digging new wells. The agreement with the
people was that villagers would dig the wells and the
missionaries would provide money to make cement
blocks to line the wells so they wouldn't cave in. Another benefit of this project was that it provided work
for many Christian men. Some were taught how to
make the curved cement blocks, and others, who had
experience in masonry, learned to line the wells with
these curved bricks. While the teams worked, they also
had opportunities to tell watching villagers about the
Living Water. And best of all, when the well was finished, Christians could model Christ in their love and
forgiveness as they announced that this water was for
everyone, not just for those who had done all the work.

Water shortage always has a negative impact on
health. Poorly nourished children and the elderly were
the first to sicken and even die. Jessie's heart ached.
Her backdoor dispensary couldn't do everything, and
one thing it certainly couldn't do was compensate for
the lack of rains and all the accompanying misery.
Jessie wrote home, "Grain for food is very short too,

and many have little or nothing to eat in the worst famine West Africa has experienced in over sixty years. In normal times the people have so little; now many have next to nothing." And with temperatures over ninety degrees in the cool of the morning, Herb and Jessie too felt the scorching heat that was tormenting their African friends.

Anyone who knew Herb knew he had an exceptionally tender heart. This was a man who was not afraid to weep. And everyone who knew him also knew he was a born entrepreneur; he knew how to make things happen. The tragedy of this famine brought out the very best in Herb. His tender heart could not bear the suffering, and his entrepreneurial drive couldn't help but find ways—big ways—to get food to the starving people he knew and loved. Beyond that, his all-consuming love for the Lord used openings gained through these acts of mercy to tell everyone about "the Jesus Road."

So Herb went looking for grain and corn. With corn costing $22 for a 200-pound sack, he wasn't able to buy very much. However, one day a truck loaded with ten tons of corn (100 sacks) pulled into his yard, a gift from a Christian relief organization. Within two days seventy-five of those bags were out in the district. Only twenty-five bags remained, but many people were still waiting for their measure of grain. One hundred sacks weren't enough.

With Herb knocking on every door to find food and then get it distributed as quickly as possible to starving people, a logistical problem facing him was the lack of storage space. Where on earth could they temporarily store this food and get it ready for distribution? He and Jessie leaned into Psalm 33:18-19: "But the eyes of the Lord are watching over those who fear him, who rely upon his steady love. He will keep them from death even in times of famine" (TLB). They mobilized friends and family to plead in prayer for relief from the suffering they saw all around them.

Each day people came by asking for grain. There were thousands upon thousands of people. In the Tougan district alone there were 220,000 people, a large majority of whom were without food. The plan was to give about ten pounds of grain per person per month, just enough to keep them from starvation. Finally, a Muslim friend of Herb's loaned him a large storeroom. Since Herb had neither time nor funds to build one, this was God's wonderful answer to prayer. But what about hauling all this grain around the district? Yes, some could be done by donkey cart, but a big vehicle was needed. Herb had once described himself as having a "big-car mentality"—a "big" man who thought "big" and asked "big" from his very "big" God. So it was no surprise to anyone when Herb's new vehicle arrived. A humanitarian agency called the World Relief Commission donated a two-ton truck which in actuality turned out to be a sturdy and economical diesel bus with twenty-two removable seats!

The bus not only served to deliver grain, but eventually it also hauled kids to camp and supplies from Bobo to construct a new classroom building near the church. It also transported the national church leaders home after their joint meeting at headquarters, hauled boards and cement and was even conscripted for ambulance duty—and much more. To this day Herb and his big bus enjoy legendary status in the memories of missionaries and nationals alike. No one who saw him hauling people and supplies all over the Tougan region will ever forget the sight nor the impression it gave of a father taking care of his large and needy family.

Even during those busy and terrible days of famine and suffering, three villages were opened to the gospel. Several Christians, sometimes pastors, sometimes Herb and national Christians, would go into a village and stay several days or up to two weeks. They preached to whoever would listen, then went from house to house to tell about Jesus' death for all, using the New Life For All evangelistic program. At the end of their visit, they would count that village as being "opened" *if* they left behind some believers. When such was the case, they'd plan return visits to teach these baby Christians and get them started walking on the Jesus Road.

About that time, Jessie got news of the passing of her mother. Jessie Ewing had visited Tougan and had been an active prayer partner in the Nehlsens' work. She prayed for pastors by name and asked her friends to do the same. Now she was gone. And in Tougan thirty pastors gathered for a short memorial service. The pastors spoke of Mrs. Ewing's prayers, giving them credit for recent conversions in their villages—six Muslims, a Tougan policeman and new conversions every Sunday for a month.

By January of 1975 the rains had returned to the parched Tougan district, and people were enjoying one of the best harvests in five years. Understandably, those who had been conditioned by famine would often try to plant in wetter, low-lying areas. But then, when the rains came in abundance, their crop would be lost to flooding. Water seemed to be both the blessing and the curse of these people Jessie and Herb loved.

Although it was nearly furlough time again, the Nehlsens were facing some unusual family circumstances. Steve was in eleventh grade and really wanted to graduate with his class. Also, during the course of the term, their beloved Becky had come out to help them for a year, and Herb had been able to make a quick trip to the U.S. to see his aged parents and Debbie. After weighing all the factors, they decided to extend their term by another year to accommodate Steve's schooling.

Steve was an excellent student (he won the student of the year award the year he graduated) and seemed to be following in his dad's footsteps by leading a weekly Bible class in French for African boys, and even, to his great delight, leading one of those boys to faith in Christ that year. When Steve was born, Herb and Jessie had asked people to pray that he would "be an instrument in the hands of the living God." They humbly thanked God for how He was answering that prayer as they watched him excel during his senior year.

What a year that extra year turned out to be! The Lord had provided for their material needs during the famine, and now He was pouring out His Spirit and providing for all sorts of spiritual needs and bringing real life and power to the Tougan area. There had been a time of seeding, using the New Life For All evangelistic tool, and now it seemed the harvest was ripening. Wherever they looked, they could see spiritual results.

A Muslim family showed up one day and asked the Nehlsens and the African pastor, François Paré, to help them with their son who seemed completely deranged. The family had tried many types of indigenous medicine and all sorts of heathen rites to no avail. The boy appeared to be hopelessly insane. Pastor Paré said he'd pray for the boy if they'd bring him to his house both morning and afternoon.

At first the boy had to be literally dragged to the house. He would say, "Where are you taking me?" When his family replied, "Into town," the boy objected. "I know where you're taking me. You're taking me to the house of the pastor who walks the Jesus Road. There are five men behind me who have warned me about this."

The boy kept coming, however, and was eventually delivered from the demons that possessed him. Although his family witnessed this deliverance, they still wanted him to take part in their Muslim fast and say his Muslim prayers, but the boy resisted. The day after his deliverance, Herb had the joy of leading him to the Lord. He kept coming to the Nehlsens wanting to learn to read so he could study the Bible himself.

Then there was the amazing story of Ali and how the Lord came to his village. Ali had once been possessed by demons who made him irrational. He too had been delivered and began praying with his wife that the good news would reach back to their home village where there were no believers. Even before Ali and his wife started praying, God was already working to answer their prayers. Although Ali didn't know it, a former military man came to know Christ and made a clean break from his Muslim past. Some years later he moved back to his village which was also Ali's original village.

One day, Herb and Jessie took a burdened Ali back to his village to share the good news. And what did they find? The village Ali remembered without a single believer now had a church attended by about twenty-five people! That same day, three more people joined the family of God. This whole story had been unfolding over a period of thirteen years, and involved several people and the work of several Christians including Herb and Jessie. The end result was something only God could have engineered—a church established in a formerly pagan village.

In 1976, the Nehlsen's term, all five years of it, was completed, and they headed to Wheaton for a twelve-month furlough. They left the people of the Tougan region in the hands of eighteen pastors, an 1,800 percent increase over the one pastor they had worked with upon their arrival just twenty years earlier. And they left a growing group of believers worshiping in the little granite-faced chapel Herb built. It was harvest time in Tougan—and the best was yet to be.

10

Monsieur Belebeleba and the Miracle Church

Two momentous occasions marked Herb and Jessie's fifth term. The first was the arrival of reinforcements. Dr. Dick and Lillian Phillips, following their victories and sufferings as missionaries in Vietnam, had come to the Tougan district to translate the Bible into the local language and also to share in the evangelization of that large district. What an encouragement this was to Herb and Jessie who had been alone for twenty years.

As Herb told of the other momentous occasion, the building of the miracle church, his face beamed and there was obvious excitement in his voice.

The little granite-faced chapel built with such faith and hard work in 1970 had now become far too small as the church body continued to grow. Herb wrote home, "The church is bulging at the seams. We never dreamed that every seat as well as the aisles would be filled in our Tougan church before it was nine years old, but that is what has happened . . . and each week there are others coming."

God seemed to have stacked His dominoes in such a way that a lot of spiritual seed-sowing in the New Life For All evangelistic campaigns and the revival of 1972 would be followed by the hard years of famine and suffering. The acts of mercy modeled by Herb and Jessie, along with the desperation that comes from living close to death, had drawn suffering Samogos in large numbers to the foot of the cross.

It was about this time that Herb and Jessie had contact with a young Canadian who was helping in agricultural development projects around Tougan. His commentary on Herb and Jessie's work is telling:

> When I first came to Upper Volta, I refused to be called a missionary. I knew I wanted to follow Jesus, but my idea of Jesus was more fashioned by liberal theology than by the living Christ of Scripture. So, I knew it was OK to share new agricultural methods and to help people in the material realm, but spiritually? I felt it was arrogance to impose my beliefs on others.
>
> Yet here before me was the example of the church in Tougan—people who had been freed through the power of Christ to live a truly different life. Their simple yet profound understanding of Scripture, and their living testimonies had, little by little, a profound effect on my life. I discovered that while I had come to share materially with them, they were filling an empty place in my spiritual being. Slowly but surely I moved from reading

Scripture with preconceived ideas to reading and submitting myself to what I read and understood. And the New Testament came alive to me, and I began to move deeper in my understanding of the Lord's will for my own life. It was then that the Lord called me to be a missionary to Africa. I, who had received new life in the cradle of the African church, was now to give back to her something of what she had nurtured in me.

Throughout the entire region churches were growing, and nowhere was that growth more evident than in the Muslim town of Tougan itself. As the chapel seemed to shrink and the need for a bigger meeting place became increasingly evident, Herb and Jessie attacked the problem as they did everything else—on their knees, with joyful hearts and hands ready to work.

The desperately poor church people also owned the burden for a larger meeting place and started saving their small sums. After seven consecutive years of famine, the people were indescribably poor, but they looked to God to provide what was needed. And they looked to the "big father" God had given them in the person of Herb.

The people called Herb "Monsieur Belebeleba—Mr. Very Big One." As Nancy Pierce, veteran missionary to Burkina Faso, said, "Everyone knew that this referred not only to his physical stature, but also to the largesse of his spirit and his pocket. His wife, Jessie, was always there at his side, matching his generosity and occasionally applying the brakes to his enthusiastic nature." As Herb tackled the construction project, it was easy to see why his moniker was perfect—Mr. Very Big One was setting out to do something huge. True to his unique style, having a dream and then moving toward realizing that dream, removing each obstacle one at a time, Monsieur Belebeleba started work on what he would forever after call "the miracle church."

And so the long process began. Land adjacent to the little chapel was bought, but nothing could be built without a building permit, and sometimes the wheels of bureaucracy move oh-so-slowly in that corner of the sub-Saharan world. Jessie and Herb had a personal reason for wanting the permit to be granted quickly. Steve, by then a student at St. Paul Bible College in Minnesota, had written to say that he wanted to be involved in the church construction. In fact, he wanted to take a semester off and bring four of his college buddies to work too.

Herb wrote back to Steve saying that if he and his friends could find the money to come, he and Jessie would give them free board and room during their stay. This was a promise he later recalled with a touch of good-natured chagrin as he and Jessie surveyed the mountains of food five young men could demolish in just one day, to say nothing of four months!

Airline reservations being what they were, Steve booked his flight even though the building permit hadn't yet been granted. To everyone's dismay, the building permit still hadn't been issued when they arrived. Had the students given up a semester for nothing?

This obstacle, however, turned out to be a God-thing. With no building permit in hand, Herb changed directions and sent his enthusiastic crew to start work on a badly needed dormitory out at Kassan's training school. This school, a center to train Christian teenagers in the rudiments of reading, writing and Bible knowledge, offered dormitories made from crumbling mud bricks and rotting thatch. Herb's dream was a new dormitory with a cement floor and a roof made with thin but sturdy sheets of metal.

Soon Steve and his pals were hard at work. Under the merciless Burkina sun, the young men made sun-dried bricks, dug dirt, pulled water from wells, hauled rocks and poured the foundation. The finished product eventually had three rooms, each one measuring fifteen by twenty feet—a spacious and comfortable answer to the school's housing needs.

Not only did Steve's and his friends' efforts produce a fine dormitory, but they also witnessed some remarkable spiritual progress. Each of these five college students had a dream. Before they left St. Paul for Africa, Steve's pastor, Dave Sohl, had urged each of them to trust the Lord for five souls on his trip. So when they arrived on Burkina soil, they were asking the Lord to give them a total of twenty-five souls for their hire. Was this just an overly enthusiastic pipe dream in the heart of a few young idealists? Time would tell.

Every weekend these young men put down their shovels and headed out to the villages to share their faith. In one new village they visited, ten men prayed and asked the King of kings to be their King. In another village four more answered the Spirit's call. And another day, Herb wrote home,

> As the sun was going down, they had their fourth service of the weekend. At the close of the service, when the national pastor gave the invitation after the fellows had sung, preached and shared their testimonies, seven stood up, indicating their desire to "walk the Jesus Road." One was the chief of the village. If you don't think that was exciting for five budding preachers, think again! "Nothing is as thrilling as seeing a soul come to Christ."

Jessie and Herb's youngest, Judi, who was spending a year in Africa before going to the States for college, worked like a trooper to help her mother feed the five workers and help with mounds of laundry each day. When the college students were ready to leave, they tallied the conversions. The number came to thirty, surpassing by five the young men's goal of twenty-five. Jessie smiled knowingly. "God gave the extra five souls for Judi because of her obedience to Him and because of all her hard work in the kitchen." Today, four of those young men are actively sharing their faith and promoting kingdom expansion—two as pastors, two as missionaries. But back to the miracle church in Tougan.

Herb was looking forward to the arrival of Glen and Marge Manske, construction experts from Rosemont Alliance Church in Lincoln, Nebraska, to help him with the massive project. To the disappointment of all, their January arrival had to be postponed. But God had planned that little wait too. Because of the delay in getting the building permit, Glen's help was needed in February, the month in which he arrived, not in January, the month he had planned to arrive.

Once again, Herb took his hammer in hand and started to build. The walls were nearly up when a torrential rain attacked the unfinished structure with incredible savagery and force. The bad news? One wall fell. The good news? Three walls held.

About that time some French Canadians arrived in Tougan to build roads in the area. They brought with them heavy-duty trucks, cement mixers and other impressive equipment that didn't exist elsewhere in Burkina. Ever hospitable, Jessie also entertained these men and their families, all the while trying to decipher the Canadian version of the French language. Herb, ever the extrovert, made friends and admired their expensive and up-to-date equipment. In the providence of God this unlikely and unexpected crossing of the ways ended up . . . well, read on.

When Herb had built the little chapel a decade earlier he had welded the girders at his house, and then the church people had gathered en masse to carry them to the church. This just wasn't possible with the massive girders now being welded to support the new church's roof; these girders were simply too heavy. But God wanted this project to happen. So Herb, never shy about asking for help from his friends, approached the French Canadians. They offered their huge truck to transport the girders the one mile from Herb's house to the church.

Then there was the problem of the roof itself. An expert Christian welder who had left Tougan two years earlier suddenly showed up and was hired to do most of the welding. Herb viewed his unexpected and amazingly timely arrival as a miracle. Herb and Jessie's colleagues, Grant and Eunice Crooks, and their son, Ken, came to help. For fifteen long working days they pounded the sheets of metal roofing tins in place.

One day, the scaffolding collapsed beneath Herb and Ken. Thankfully, tragedy was averted as they were able to grab onto the I-beams sixteen feet in the air while other workers scrambled to help them. Shaken but unhurt, Herb and Ken were soon putting the scaffolding back together and climbing back up.

Laying a 3,000-square-foot cement floor was the next mammoth stage of the construction process. How many women would need to carry how many buckets of water on their heads to make enough cement? The figure was too astronomical to even contemplate. Herb started to calculate, then shook his head. He decided to go calling on the French Canadians again! The result? One Saturday the Canadian road builders maneuvered their heavy equipment into the churchyard. Before they left, the entire cement floor lay shiny and smooth in the late afternoon light— a glistening mammoth miracle.

Just as Herb had put granite feature columns and a cross on the front of Tougan's first chapel, he wanted the outside of this big church to look attractive too. He had an idea, but he'd be needing a lot of help if it were ever to become a reality. Entrepreneur that he was, Herb never lacked for contacts. One of those contacts led him to a Muslim millionaire in the capital city. Never shy, Herb went to see this follower of Allah and asked for help in getting some good granite to make stucco.

"Of course I'll get some for you," the man responded. "And you," he said, gesturing to an employee, "write 'paid' on the invoice. This is for a House of God where you will pray to God; you must have the very best. My crew are experts at applying this kind of stucco. I'll send them to Tougan to do the job for you."

And he did! The crew finished work just one-and-a-half hours before the start of the weekend celebrations planned to dedicate the building to Herb and Jessie's incredible God! But the drama of the construction and the visible beauty of the church was not the real importance of that building. The first service of the dedication weekend featured the powerful testimony of a converted Muslim businessman. Glancing around at the impressive structure in which they were seated, he encouraged everyone, especially young people, to make their bodies God's dwelling place. And by the time he was done preaching, no one there thought the new building was anything but a shelter in which to worship the living God. Everyone recognized that God's true house is in people's hearts.

During the dedication service itself, field chairman David Kennedy reminded the little group that they had once worshiped under a cornstalk shelter that seemed so big at the time. But praise God! In less than a decade, they had outgrown that shelter and also the little chapel. David challenged the congregation of "living stones" to keep growing as an alive and witnessing church.

Today, Herb's miracle church stands tall and proud in Tougan, Burkina Faso. On special Sundays, all its shiny cement benches are filled with more than 600 people pressed together like cards in a deck. Even the aisles are blocked with worshipers perched on grass mats. It is the hub of Christian life in that Muslim city of 10,000 people.

Herb and Jessie's God had truly done a miracle in Tougan—with a little help from Monsieur Belebeleba.

11

At the Mere Mention of His Name

Herb just loved to tour in churches during furlough. Meeting people, talking about Africa, eating delicious and extra-special meals especially prepared for the visiting missionary, speaking in churches—all this was Herb's meat and drink both literally and figuratively. As he traveled and spoke, his purpose never wavered. He wanted people to pray for the Tougan area. He wanted to find new missionary recruits. He wanted to raise money for Tougan's many needs.

One of his favorite tours was in Montana. Many of the churches were small, and he would often be the only missionary. The preliminaries were minimal, and then they'd turn the rest of the time over to Herb. He could take as much time as he wanted. It was great! People were drawn to this big man with the tender heart. He'd tell famine stories with tears rolling down his cheeks. People would listen, open their wallets and promise to pray for Tougan. On this particular furlough after his sixth term, he was given a new welder, a wind charger, a generator, water pumps, basic medical supplies, fabric Bible covers and book bags for students, bags of baby clothes for needy newborns, canned food . . . and more. The list went on and on. All this would mean a hefty duty bill later, but Herb and Jessie knew they could attack that problem with the help of their prayer partners and with the limitless resources of their heavenly Father.

Laura Livingston, Alliance missionary to Côte d'Ivoire, who became one of Herb and Jessie's recruits during their previous furlough, wrote later:

> Uncle Herb and Aunt Jessie . . . took pity on this poor newly married couple and fed us generously and often. Aunt Jessie's delicious cooking was served up in equal portions with Uncle Herb's burden for the lost of West Africa. His claim that we don't need a call to go where the need is endless, [but] we need a call to stay where the work is well supplied was the first step on our road to overseas ministry.
>
> On their next furlough, Herb called us from a pay phone, "What are you still doing in North America? Get your friends together. We'll have a missions meeting tonight." And complete with a snake skin longer than our tiny living room and the inevitable tears for the lost, we had missions with Uncle Herb. The Nehlsens helped supply our outfit, Herb preached our commissioning service message and we went to West Africa together.

Their prayers and encouragement have been the background to all our eighteen years in missions. They counseled, prayed, loved, gave generously and always wrapped us up in arms of warm hospitality. They loved our children as their own (giving rise to a nasty fight when their real granddaughter informed our little girl that Grandma Jessie was not really hers!). They cried with us when our wretched car broke down yet again and when I was evacuated twice with serious illnesses and when our newborn danced on the edge of death in her early months.

Above all, they have kept our eyes turned to that Jesus, the mere mention of whose name brings tears to Herb's eyes. If we have accomplished anything by God's grace, it began with their challenge and will finish in the light of their encouragement.

On one occasion during that furlough, a pastor was wringing his hands over the no-show of a speaker during his missionary convention. Someone asked him if another missionary had been assigned to take his place. When he replied, "Herb Nehlsen," there was a chuckle and the advice, "Then you don't have anything to worry about. Give Herb the whole time; his stories can stretch to fill any amount of time!" It was true. Herb's stories were captivating, but when he spoke of Jesus or the Samogo, his eyes would fill with tears and the emotion of this gentle giant would move his audiences to a greater commitment to His wonderful Lord.

That furlough came to an end, and with great anticipation Jessie and Herb drove back up that long road to
Tougan once again. The churches had grown. New villages had been opened. Taking advantage of that mo-
mentum, they kept on with their local ministries but
also seized opportunities to do more evangelism in the
region. Herb always made sure that his prayer partners
understood that evangelism was to be a priority. Why?
There were several reasons, he said: 1) it was the final
command of Him who loved us and gave Himself for
us; 2) so many still haven't heard—hundreds of villages
remain without one believer; and 3) people's hearts
are more open than ever before to listen, and the Holy
Spirit is convincing them of their need of a Savior.

It was the dry month of March in the town of
Solenzo, a government center where there was a tiny
church and great spiritual need. The national church
and the Mission decided to send a team of evangelists to target this Muslim town. The church put five
pastors gifted in evangelism on the team, and the
Mission sent Jessie, Herb and fellow missionary Bob
Kauffman. Jessie later reported:

> We experienced a few inconveniences such
> as daily temperatures over 100 degrees,
> sleeping on camp cots and taking splash
> baths, and our cool water supply running out
> soon after we arrived. But any lack of physi-
> cal comfort was more than made up by the
> joy we experienced in sharing God's Good
> News in the mornings as we went out two by
> two throughout the town and in the evenings
> as large crowds came to listen and to see a

Christian film. Many times people we had talked with that day came to make a decision at night. Afternoons found us having classes for some of these new converts and selling literature.

One of those who made a decision had come from a nearby village and wanted the team of evangelists to go back home with him to help him burn his fetishes. What a celebration it was as he stood by the fire and sang in his own language, "Jesus has freed us, let us all tell it; Jesus has freed us, it's a miracle!" Five people who were watching decided they too wanted to walk the Jesus Road. The next day another fifteen converted, and then one more fetisher left his false religion behind.

Some months later, when Herb and Jessie were hosting a team of college students from the U.S., Herb decided to take the students to that village to see how the baby church was faring. The new believers and many others came out to listen as the team preached, sang and showed a film. As the service continued, Herb and the college students were praying with all the faith they could muster that God would hold off the torrential storm threatening to close in all around them.

God answered. They were able to have both an afternoon and evening service albeit surrounded by storm clouds and lightning. It soon became obvious that, while they were worshiping, other villages had re-

ceived torrential rains, for as they drove home they av-
eraged fourteen miles an hour through a sea of water.

The church in Solenzo continued to move ahead,
and a few months later Jessie and Rebecca, an African
pastor's wife and Jessie's close friend, arrived to hold a
women's conference there. This was just one of many
women's conferences Jessie and Rebecca led. They'd
go to different villages at prearranged times, and
women would gather at the church and stay for several
days, even a week. They each paid a small fee that covered food costs. Jessie and Rebecca would speak in the
teaching sessions on basic themes like how to have assurance of salvation, how to have a Christian family
and how to experience the fullness of the Spirit in their
lives. Women's hearts were changed. And at Solenzo,
an elder's wife became a Christian, and a pastor's wife
received assurance of her salvation. Even though
Jessie and Herb had the spiritual gift of evangelism,
they never saw it as a gift which stood alone. They understood that Christians would not grow unless evangelism was followed by teaching the Word of God. So
whenever they went out evangelizing, they never failed
to plan return visits to bring scriptural instruction to
new and older believers alike.

Jessie also continued her work in the dispensary
along with her trusted aide, Teresa. When Teresa's
husband took sick and died, Herb and the local pastor
handled the funeral. An influential nephew of the dead
man, a colonel in the army, arrived for the service. After the funeral, Saye Zerbo made a point of thanking
Herb for doing such a fine job. Although he was a
Muslim, he appreciated the Protestant arrangements.

Not long after that, Saye Zerbo's daughter, a high school student, burned her leg on her motorbike and came to Jessie's dispensary for treatment. Soon this teenager, along with her younger sister, had become Christians and they were both baptized. But the story doesn't end there. In the meantime, Saye Zerbo, who was becoming very powerful in the army, ousted his uncle from the presidency and took over himself as president of Burkina Faso.

"Hey, guess what! I talked to the president of the country last week!" Herb's big face beamed with delight as he bragged to his fellow missionaries.

"Oh, Herb, get serious! You're such a joker," they responded in essence.

"No, it's true!" Herb insisted as he went on to tell them the whole story of how he had driven one of the pastors to see the president's guard to whom he was related. The president welcomed them warmly and served them a drink.

Saye Zerbo's tenure ended when he too was ousted in a military takeover, and he was placed under house arrest. When his Muslim friends saw he had fallen from grace, they deserted him. The Catholic friends he had because of his Catholic wife followed suit. Now he was alone, deserted by his followers, but not by God. A local clergyman came to visit him and presented him with a Bible. Saye started to read the Scriptures. He read and read and then read some more. His thirst for the Word of God seemed insatiable. In fact, during his house arrest he read the Bible cover to cover four times. Herb had the opportunity to visit him and, after a discussion, the two

men prayed and Saye confessed the faith that had already taken root in his heart.

While still under house arrest, he was moved from
the capital to his house in Tougan where he continued
to study the Bible. One time when Herb went to visit
him, he had four Bibles spread out in front of him and
was comparing one version with another. The soldiers
guarding him often brought him newspapers, but he
preferred the Bible and would put the papers aside to
study the Scripture. The Lord revealed many things to
Saye during those days. For one thing, he felt the Lord
told him he wouldn't have to go to prison. Yet one day
soldiers arrived to take him there. They escorted him
to the prison, signed him in and gave him his cell number. Just then a worker came to the desk saying that
the lightbulb in Saye's cell had burned out. The worker
was sent to buy a new bulb. While he was gone, an order came saying Saye was to be returned to his house
in Tougan. He had heard the Lord correctly— he did-
n't have to go to prison.

Saye's first wife was a woman with little formal education. When Saye came to the Lord, he was very gentle with this unsophisticated woman and never forced
her to leave her Muslim ways. But one day, during the
one-month fast observed by all Muslims, his wife had a
vision. She went to Saye, and after telling him her vision, they talked until he was able to lead her to the
Savior. His other wife was from the royal family, a
highly educated and cultured woman of the Mossi
tribe. She too became a Christian, and when she saw
other women going to Bible studies at the church, she
said, "I'm going to learn to read and write Jula so I can

study the Bible with these women." And learn it she did, even though for a Mossi to learn Jula wasn't a prestigious thing to do.

Time went on until a significant day arrived, the day Saye Zerbo wanted to declare his faith in Christ publicly by passing though the waters of baptism. As he came out of the water, this former Muslim, this former president of Burkina Faso, raised both hands and shouted, "Hallelujah!" Later, at the big party he hosted to celebrate the occasion, Herb raised a glass of tonic water to his lips and reminded Saye of the first tonic they had drunk together while Saye was still a Muslim. God had worked a miracle and brought this influential man and his family to express faith in Jesus Christ openly. At the time of this writing, Saye Zerbo is alive and living in the capital city of Burkina, Ouagadougou (wah-ga-DOO-goo). He worships regularly at the Alliance church, always arriving early. Before the days when there was a French church service, this important but humble man would come and worship in Jula.

Another mature man met the Lord about then too, much to Herb and Jessie's great delight. Herb explains,

> The next Sunday, when I was visiting the church in Sienna, we had a great time of fellowship in the worship service, singing and praising the Lord. Then, in the afternoon I felt led to go and visit the old, old father of the elder in charge of that church. The Christians there told me many had witnessed to him without any success, but we could go again if I wanted.

I went with a good interpreter since I don't know the southern Samogo language. We prayed for God's Spirit to go before us. After my presentation, the father said, "We agree, this is the way. We will be in church next Sunday morning to let folks know we are walking the Jesus Road."

What was I hearing? Did he really understand my words? It had been too easy! So I explained again as clearly as I could, telling him he would have to leave his fetishes, no longer worship any idols and only worship Jesus. But in a very powerful, positive way he said, "I understand all you have said. I will be in church next Sunday morning to announce that I have accepted Christ."

Wow! That was something God had done. Then I asked about his wife, and he said, "She'll be there with me. We are both coming."

Hallelujah! So we prayed with this elderly man, and we went back to join the others, rejoicing with the angels in heaven. When we reported this good news in the Sunday evening service, everyone rejoiced. One of the women came to me after and told me she had been praying for the salvation of four people. Three had accepted Christ, this old man was the one remaining person, but now he too had come. What a day of rejoicing that was for her.

Later, the old man sent word that it was getting cool, and he needed a used overcoat to keep warm, and since I was his father would I please send one to him. Jessie and I were delighted to buy a used coat in the market and send it to him.

Despite encouragements like this old man's and Saye's conversion, Herb and Jessie recognized that their load was becoming too heavy. Their responsibilities just kept on multiplying. When Jessie was home, she still had seventy to eighty patients a day at her backdoor dispensary. In addition, there was the preparation she needed to do for teaching at the girls' school and the women's conferences. So it was with a heart of deep gratitude to the Lord and to the Mission that Herb and Jessie opened their hearts and their home to two new missionaries from Holland, Jetty Stouten and Joke Blumink. These women, both nurses, started studying the Jula language while slowly taking over the medical work and some teaching jobs from Jessie. An additional blessing was Joke's willingness to do much-needed dental care in that isolated part of the country where dentists were as scarce as hen's teeth!

While this was going on, the famine was worsening again. The Nehlsens, as well as other missionaries, were doing all they could to get food to starving people and to get wells dug in the many villages without water. Herb wrote home, "The constant prayer from our hearts is that the many, many hours spent in grain distribution and overseeing the digging of wells will clearly testify of God's love and bring glory to Him."

The people's great needs and their gratitude for grain and wells seemed to make them more open to the gospel. Scores of people came to Christ every year. This meant baptism classes and then, for each new church, the very first baptismal service. Herb was often called for such an important occasion. Near one particular village there wasn't much water. The few little waterholes they managed to find were slimy and green. Herb, however, didn't back out. Pea soup or not, he had the privilege of baptizing people who had placed their faith and trust in the true and living God.

The Nehlsens' family also saw some interesting developments that term. Steve married Amy; their first grandchild, Debbie's Andrea (Peck), was born, and Becky did a term of missionary work in Zaire. All these wonderful things seemed like showers of blessing to Jessie and Herb as they persisted in that physically and spiritually dry and thirsty land.

As their busiest and most demanding term yet drew to a close, an old man for whom they had prayed since 1968 opened his heart to Christ.

"What greater joy could there be than that!" Herb wrote. "Better than a great grain harvest that we pray for, greater than wells full of water is the joy of a life that surrenders to Christ. This dear old man can say with the psalmist, 'I will lie down and sleep in peace.' He is safe in the fold. Hallelujah!"

12

Marks of Greatness

A dusty little village. A crude cornstalk shelter. A small group of less than twenty-five adults. Cheek-splitting smiles. Tears of joy. Loud, rhythmic singing. The occasion was a happy one, the arrival of the church's very first pastor. Herb and Jessie were there to deliver Pastor Moses and his wife to this tiny body of believers at the First Alliance Church of Seme (SAY may).

Overwhelmed with their good fortune, the people rejoiced. They now had their own pastor! None of them could read or write, but the Spirit of God was living in them, and they wanted to know more and more about Him. Now they had a shepherd to teach them. They would no longer have to rely on the occasional visits of an itinerant preacher. Their pastor would teach them to read and write too, and he'd be their spiritual chief, a source of security for the little flock.

With overflowing hearts they made an enormous gesture of appreciation, the appropriate thing in that culture—they presented Herb with a sheep. Big Herb, standing there with his head slightly bent out of respect for the low ceiling, could hardly bear that moment. These poor, illiterate men and women, with both spiritual and physical hunger showing on every gaunt face, were so thankful to him, the humble servant of God who had made sure Seme and villages like it heard the good news.

Herb accepted their gift that day. It was the appropriate thing to do. Then he leaned into the hard work of getting more grain to the hungry, helping more people find work, digging more wells, ordering more medicines, driving more people where they needed to go, finding more young leaders to send to the Bible institute, teaching more pastors truths from the Word. More, more, more. That was the story of Herb and Jessie's life.

Herb and Jessie were getting older though, and now they found themselves heading into the last term of their missionary career. Earlier, as they were packing and preparing to return to Africa for the last time, they wrote their friends,

> Letters coming from Burkina Faso tell us that June planting is still being done in August. A harvest will take a miracle. Pray. This could mean heavy relief ministries again this year. But let us never forget that their greatest hunger is spiritual. There are 140 villages in our area waiting to hear about the Bread of Life. Will you pray for a harvest in Burkina Faso? A grain harvest, yes, but especially a harvest of souls for eternity?

Herb and Jessie's fears were realized. They returned to find the worst drought they had seen yet. Many people had harvested only enough to feed their family for a month or two. As a result, young men and even church elders migrated south to find work until the next farming season. This was tough in a region that always needed more church leaders.

Once again the Nehlsens found themselves distributing grain, but they simply couldn't buy enough to satisfy the great needs all around them. They had to set priorities: widows, the aged, handicapped people and pastors who had total crop failure. Wherever he went, Herb tried to buy grain which he would then give away to the destitute. Sometimes he could buy grain from Ghana or from some other area, and sometimes he could even buy imported Canadian wheat.

When grain was available, Herb just loved projects called "food for work." He'd find a project in the community that needed doing and then tell people they could report for work and would be paid in grain. One such community project was a road that needed repair. Herb had always felt the Lord had put that particular road in so they could go up north to preach the gospel. Now the food-for-work project was fixing up a bridge so they could keep going north and keep evangelizing the area.

Herb liked this way of getting food to hungry people. It had the distinct advantage of avoiding the handout method which could eat away at self-esteem. And the added blessing was seeing projects completed which helped the entire community. Everyone would come—men, women, children, donkey carts and all. With grain as the payment, they showed up.

Enrollment at the training school in Kassan was also affected by the drought since many young people didn't have enough grain, the currency they needed in order to pay the tuition for their three-year program of reading, writing, Bible, a little mathematics and basic hygiene. Despite the lower enrollment, thirty girls completed their studies the first year after the Nehlsens' return and tucked a new Bible into their bundles as they returned home. The girls who succeeded in their studies had the coveted opportunity to buy a Bible at half price, a real incentive to work hard.

As soon as they moved out, twenty-one boys moved into the solid dormitories built by Steve Nehlsen and his friends. That's how the school scheduled itself every year. Jessie and Herb saw this school tucked away in the little village of Kassan as an important part of discipleship in the area and a feeder for the Bible school program. Jessie was there every week with her lessons in basic health education, and she, along with Herb, kept an eye on the students, eager to encourage any whom God would call to be pastors.

Despite the desperate times, Herb's chauffeuring service delivered eight more students, the pastors of tomorrow, along with their wives, to Bible school that year. Two years later, this number had grown to fourteen couples and two single men. Herb wrote home, "We're trying to help where we can; with so many churches without pastors, we believe this (actively seeking out and then sending serious young Christians to the Bible institute) is a worthwhile investment."

Older pastors too were upgrading both their knowledge of the Bible and their teaching skills. They had this opportunity to study thanks to an instruction method called Theological Education by Extension (TEE). Pastors and lay leaders would study at home and then every week or two meet in small groups with a facilitator. The benefit of this system was that mature people, mostly men, didn't have to leave their homes and fields to study at a residential Bible school. They could study in their own villages and immediately apply the scriptural truths they learned in the small churches they were leading. Both Herb and Jessie taught courses and encouraged others to train to be facilitators.

As usual, church construction was a high priority for Herb. Five sheet-metal roofs went on five different churches in the Tougan area during the first part of that last term. A special delight for both Herb and Jessie was seeing a new church go up in the village of Toma. Herb always said Toma was a hard place to work. In the early days, when he'd go there to sell books, youth and children would come and spit at him and even throw a few stones. As he commented, "When this happened several times, you knew you were not wanted." But he persisted, and eventually he found a lay pastor willing to live there and try to start a church. They rented a house for him and asked him to locate a piece of property to buy. After many attempts, he found a nice lot, and a team of Christians, including Herb, went to Toma to build a small chapel and a house for the pastor. It was hard work. They had to make mud bricks and dry them in the sun, but some

townspeople refused to give them water from their
wells to make the bricks. Others chased them out of
the fields where they had gone to get mud to make the
bricks.

One day, as Herb was working on that tiny chapel,
he looked across the street to a large piece of property, and the Lord gave him a vision. In his spirit he
saw a much bigger church sitting on that site for the
glory of God. So, for ten long years Herb watched
the efforts of the few struggling Christians in Toma.
And always, he thought of his vision.

The Phillipses, now living in Toma, were busily en-
gaged in translation ministries. But these two weren't
stay-at-home linguists. On weekends they were out
working in and around Toma, trying to establish a
strong church there. Lillian too had a backdoor dispensary where the love she dispensed along with her
medicine spoke volumes to the people of Toma.

God chose to honor this hard work, prayer and
faithfulness until finally a growing number of believers
had outgrown the original chapel. The search was on
for a larger lot where a more spacious church could be
built. Those were still famine years, and the chief in
Toma was also feeling the effects of drought. He
needed money, so he agreed to sell a lot to the church,
and yes, he sold the very piece of land Herb had seen
in his vision!

Once again, Herb happily took on the job of building the new church; he put on the roof with the help of
two other missionaries. At last the new church was finished. But wait: Herb had another errand. He went
back to the first little chapel in Tougan and took its

cross, the one he had once carefully welded out of scrap metal, and transported it to Toma. The old welded cross was installed on the front of the new Toma church—a recycled cross, a powerful symbol of eternal hope.

Today, believers in the Toma church are God's presence and light in that hard place. The Phillipses finished the New Testament, and other Scripture portions and materials they translated are being proclaimed and taught in both Toma and the entire region. After the Phillipses' retirement, a translation team continued working to produce the entire Bible in the San language. Someday Herb and Jessie's beloved Samogo people will have the complete Word in their own mother tongue.

The Nehlsens' Tougan clock was starting to run down. Several factors in their lives were indicating a new lap in the marathon of their career. For one thing, the Tougan region was seeing new pastors trained every year. These pastors were sharing Herb and Jessie's vision to get the Word to every one of the area's 220 villages. The Nehlsens were working as hard as ever, but in many respects they had already successfully multiplied themselves many times over.

The missionary cliché applied to them—they had worked themselves out of a job! They never saw it quite that way though. As long as there was even one village without Christ, they had work to do: evangelizing, discipling, healing the sick, sending teenagers to Kassan's school and finding likely candidates to go to the Bible institute. Another factor too was coming into play. Herb was increasingly sought out to lead the Alliance missionaries as they worked alongside their African counterparts. He had become an elder. His wisdom and experience were recognized and valued. A respected colleague, an elder like himself, Milt Pierce said of Herb,

> Herb really had the "marks of greatness." He was . . . an unusual individual . . . a man of great faith, great vision, great compassion, great heart. In the Nehlsens' years of ministry among the San people they left behind one of the strongest district churches in Burkina. Herb was a teacher, both from the Book and by example. He gave himself without reserve to the work of the ministry.
>
> The Nehlsens were a rare combination of spiritual zeal and social concern. They fed the hungry, ministered to the sick and cared for the poor. They were in some ways the last of a generation of missionaries that gave themselves for a lifetime to village evangelism. It was fitting that near the end of their career Herb was called upon to be director of the mission for two years. God always seems to have His man for such a ministry and at the time needed. Herb took over at a time when the Burkina Mission desperately needed his compassionate heart, his steady hand and long experience. He was able to deal graciously with the national church president and to guide the mission through some trying years.

A young missionary told of her memorable encounter with this giant of faith. She had the unenviable task of driving herself and her three small children, in a car that wasn't running properly, to meet her husband who was waiting several hours away. Hearing her talk about her unreliable car, Herb couldn't keep silent. With a warm hug, he challenged her, "Where's your faith? Pray and ask God for a Mercedes station wagon and then sit back and see how He answers!" The new missionary's faith didn't net her a Mercedes, but she was able to find someone to accompany her and eventually found herself safely reunited with her husband.

Tales like those are legion. With such a reputation, Herb and Jessie had two new opportunities come to them. First, they were sent to Guinea's capital city of Conakry to direct the Mission there during the field director's furlough (see chapter 13). Later, they were sent to Burkina Faso's headquarters to lead its team of fifty-two missionaries. Herb had sought neither job and hated to leave the work in the Tougan area, but he and Jessie had always been submissive to directives from Mission leaders. Although they would have never chosen to move twice during their last term, they accepted these changes as from the hand of God and faced them with their usual combination of contagious joy coupled with a deep and abiding faith in God.

After the Guinea saga, in 1990, they moved back to Burkina Faso, to the city of Bobo Dioulasso where the Mission office is located. However, as might be predicted, instead of an executive job in air-conditioned comfort, Herb found himself finishing construction of the new compound. The original one, built in 1923, had been traded to the national church for a spacious property far away from the center of town. The new compound would eventually include an office building, workshop, storage buildings, a duplex and the field director's residence.

One question that came up during construction was whether or not to put a cement wall between the director's house and the office building. Predictably, Herb, who had planted over 200 trees around his Tougan house, cast his vote for trees and then got busy planting them. Herb and Jessie, who for a couple of decades had had a public dispensary just outside their kitchen door, were happiest without walls separating them from other people.

As the field director's wife, Jessie managed the portfolio of station hostess. With great cooking skills and a big heart, she graciously received any and all who arrived at her door. Her last Christmas in Burkina Faso, with retirement just six months away, she welcomed some very special people. All her children and grandchildren arrived for Herb and Jessie's last Burkina Christmas. Those children were adults now. Becky had held various positions since college including a term in Zaire as bookkeeper and guest-house manager for The Christian and Missionary Alliance. Later, choosing a career as a flight attendant, she made it possible for Herb and Jessie to fly free to many different destinations in the United States and even overseas.

Debbie, the Nehlsens' second child, married Larry Peck and had given Herb and Jessie two grandchildren, Andrea and Nathan. Debbie wrote, "For eight months I baked for Café Zog (on the east side of Providence, Rhode Island) as I tried to earn $5,000 to get our family to Africa for my parents' last Christmas." When she later published a cookbook, O *Taste and See*, (Jumbo Jack's Cookbooks, Audubon Media Corporation, Audubon, IA 50025), which included many recipes from her two sisters, she dedicated it to her parents: "This book is lovingly dedicated to my parents, Herb and Jessie Nehlsen. Mom gave me a love for cooking. Dad gave me a love for eating. Together they gave me a love for God and His Kingdom." Debbie's goal for publishing the cookbook was to raise funds for her family's move to Italy where Larry would be teaching at the Italian Bible Institute outside of Rome. The Pecks moved to Italy in 1999.

Judi too brought immeasurable joy to her parents' hearts. She also was a gourmet cook and a hard worker. When Herb headed into his final retirement, one of his dreams was to take over the handyman role in Judi's newly purchased house. Herb and Jessie were planning to retire in North Carolina but, thanks to Becky's airline tickets, they could frequently spend time with Judi in Florida.

And Steve? What about Herb and Jessie's only living son about whom they had prayed and had asked others to pray that he'd be an instrument in the hands of the living God? With deep gratitude and humility, Jessie and Herb recognized that those prayers were being answered to the glory of God. Steve had stayed true to his childhood faith through high school, college and graduate school. Amy, the beautiful and talented wife he chose, was from a godly home and shared his unswerving commitment to kingdom expansion. To no one's surprise, Steve and Amy ended up as missionaries of The Christian and Missionary Alliance, working among Jula people, Muslims, in Bouaké, Côte d'Ivoire. Amy and Steve added more grandchildren to the extended Nehlsen family—Abigail, Kari and Peter. (Baby Samuel James was buried in African soil on April 1, 1991.)

Although the Christmas festivities took place in Bobo Dioulasso where Herb and Jessie were living, the entire crew made a memorable trip back to Tougan to see the familiar faces and places of the children's growing up years.

A few months later, before retiring to the U.S., Herb and Jessie returned one last time to Tougan.

> Our friends there wanted to have our farewell service as part of their annual ladies' conference, so they invited all of the pastors and many of the church leaders. Both of us shared in the ministry of the conference. Smiles and tears were mingled often during those days as we said good-bye to dear friends we don't expect to see until we get to heaven. Praise God with us that many Samogos will be present when Christ calls His bride to Himself. Hallelujah!

Retirement. The celebration of thirty-seven years of missionary service. The big day was approaching. Jessie and Herb were sure that none of their daughters would be there to help celebrate, but they were anticipating a happy time with their Burkina missionary family. From past experience they knew the missionaries would have a memorable (and hilarious) farewell planned for them featuring skits and delicious refreshments. In addition Steve and Amy, along with little Abby, would attend. What they didn't know was that Becky had secretly made plans to surprise them by arriving the day before the retirement party. Thanks to the complicity of willing missionaries, she was met at the airport and then driven to the conference center where the party was held. With a delighted smile, she walked into the room where her parents were. Now Herb and Jessie could enjoy even more of the evening planned by their colleagues. One highlight of that event was receiving a very unusual gift from their missionary friends—a poster-sized portrait of themselves burned onto suede leather.

The *Alliance Video Magazine* also highlighted the Nehlsens' thirty-seven-year ministry with a short video clip focusing on the famine years. A middle-aged Jessie could be seen dispensing medicine and teaching her patients. And Herb, driving his big twenty-two-seat Saviem, talking loudly over the engine's noise, was telling about the tragedy of the drought and how he was able to help with grain and wells thanks to donors back home. At the end of the video clip, the camera zoomed in for a closeup of Herb's face, twisted with emotion, tears trickling down his craggy cheeks. This moving image portrayed for all the world to see the tremendous love Herb and Jessie had poured out during their years in Africa—a love and concern which hadn't diminished with time.

Jessie and Herb's first prayer when they came to Africa had been, "Lord, keep our hearts tender, burdened, caring that people are lost." The Lord had heard their prayer, and for nearly forty years their hearts had been full of loving compassion for the lost souls all around them.

But retirement didn't spell "the end" for this energetic couple. Instead, they would return to Africa for shorter terms and in locations other than their beloved Tougan. In fact, after their furlough year they returned to Africa not once, not twice, but three times.

> God does not lead us year by year,
>   Nor even day by day.
> But step by step our paths unfold
>   As He directs our way.
> Tomorrow's plans are never sure;
>   We only know this minute.
> But He will say, "This is the way,
>   By faith, now walk ye in it."

—Author unknown. Excerpted from "Nehlsen News," February, 1989.

13

The King of Bear Hugs and the Queen of Encouragement

It was the last straw! On one of his many errands to downtown Conakry, Guinea, Herb was tracking down a visa needed by a missionary. In a hurry, tired and irritated, he had parked in his usual spot. But this time, a short man whose military clothes proclaimed him to have some authority was bound and determined to extract a bribe—and a little respect—out of the big American sweating in front of him.

I don't have time for this, Herb thought. *But if I call his bluff and he reports me to his superiors I could end up wasting the entire morning.* The wheels started turning, and a plan began to take shape somewhere in the back of his head. Before he knew it, he moved in front of the soldier, dropped to his knees and in a loud voice pleaded with the startled man to forgive him. The soldier, stunned, stood paralyzed with amazement. Never in his career had he encountered anything like this! Without further ado, he pointed Herb back into his car, thrust his car documents at him and then, holding up his hand to stop the traffic and let Herb through, he waved the relieved missionary on his way.

Although Herb and Jessie were Burkina missionaries, they had been pressed into service on the Guinea field. Guinea's field director was going on furlough, and the Nehlsens had been asked to fill in for the year of his absence.

It wasn't easy to step into such a position, particularly on a field that was not their own. Both Herb and Jessie would need all the faith and ingenuity they possessed to succeed. Their assignment included caring for Mission business, managing the guest house, preaching occasionally at the International Church and overseeing the work of the Alliance missionaries in Guinea. Not only was that more than two people could realistically be expected to do, but the Guinea field was also in a time of great transition. After years of restrictions due to a Marxist regime, the country was finally offering missionaries freedom to do their work as they wished. The Alliance office in North America responded aggressively by sending one new missionary after another to this mostly Muslim country. During just one year, Herb and Jessie welcomed one woman missionary and four young families.

As Herb and Jessie struggled with water cuts, power outages and multiple thefts at their compound, they thought longingly of the simple life they had left behind in Tougan and felt great admiration and empathy for the new missionaries launching their careers in such a difficult spot. These young missionaries became like their own children, and they supported them in every way possible. One of them wrote:

> We had had the typical terrible first-term experience and were doubting we'd ever come back to Guinea. But just at that point into our lives walked the king of bear hugs and the queen of encouragement.
>
> They showed us we didn't have to live such a spartan life; it was OK to have water towers, and it was OK to have 12-volt lights (we had neither running water nor electricity our first term). Herb even showed us how to set all this up. They encouraged us to live a lifestyle that would enable us to be in Guinea for a lifetime.
>
> When my husband was so sick with hepatitis, all he craved was bran muffins. Where in the world would I get bran? Jessie heard the Lord's small voice, baked bran muffins and then drove two hours upcountry to deliver them to my yellow but awestruck husband. We hadn't said a thing to anyone about this obsession with muffins, yet Jessie was there just at the right moment with just what he wanted.
>
> Our hearts were broken by the love Herb and Jessie showed the lost Muslims of Guinea. On several trips Herb would weep as we drove through countless villages where the Muslims there would never even once in their lives have the chance to hear about Jesus. Those trips were what mentoring is all

about as we began to see Muslims as Herb
and the Lord saw them. It was impossible for
him to pray for lost Muslims without break-
ing into tears. This great big guy had the
most tender heart we'd ever seen.

But life in Conakry seemed to be one annoying
thing after another. When the wire carrying electricity into the guest house was repeatedly stolen,
Herb's solution was to buy pieces of wire and splice
them together, knowing that the spliced wire wasn't
nearly as attractive to thieves. And hearing the
phone ring always startled the Nehlsens since the
telephone was so rarely functional.

The Christian and Missionary Alliance was about
the only Mission with official status in the country at
that time. As a result, the Alliance umbrella covered
four other Missions who wanted to work in Guinea—
the Southern Baptists, Campus Crusade, the Canadian Pentecostal Mission and Pioneer Bible Translators. Jessie, with her gift of hospitality, and Herb, with
his gift of helps, were exactly the right people for that
job that year. They provided a safe haven, a good laugh
and practical advice along with a fine cup of coffee to
all these new missionaries coming to their door.

Before leaving Tougan, Jessie had wondered what
her ministry in Guinea would be. The language spoken
in Conakry differed from the Jula she knew, and for
the first time in her life she'd be living in a yard surrounded by a wall. Further, she wouldn't have her
backdoor dispensary to give her contacts with the
neighbors. As she prayed, the Lord clearly showed her
that her unique ministry would be hospitality. And so

she tackled her new role in Jesus' name, entertaining missionaries, taking care of carloads of kids on their way to boarding school, comforting a young mother who had just sent her first child away to school and even helping to evacuate a critically ill missionary woman.

Both Herb and Jessie were deeply burdened for the Muslims they saw all around them in Conakry and the outlying areas. They gave themselves to pray for these people and never quit even after they left Guinea. They followed Guinea's spiritual progress as the missionaries there focused on three specific people groups resistant to the gospel—the Fulani, the Maninka and the Susu. Each of these groups meant something special to Herb and Jessie. They saw the young missionaries in their care, their adopted children, take on very demanding ministry assignments among these three people groups, all predominantly Muslim. Along with these young missionaries, their hearts resonated to the incredible need of the 2.5 million Fulani living in Guinea. They knew this to be Guinea's largest unreached people group. How their hearts rejoiced as the work steadily moved ahead there until, at the beginning of the new millennium, long after Herb and Jessie had left, there were two groups of believers worshiping on a regular basis.

The Maninka had a special place in their prayers because, besides being Guinea's second largest group of people resistant to the gospel, they were also closely related to the people group targeted by Steve and Amy in Côte d'Ivoire. Although believers numbered fewer than a handful in Guinea, by the time Herb and Jessie faced retirement, there was the beginning of several small Bible studies.

The Susu people were the third group regularly brought before the throne of Jessie and Herb's big God. And, as they prayed for over a decade, God started to work and brought into being a Susu Church. Tiny, struggling, needy in every way, the Susu Bride of Christ is alive today in that Guinean context.

After fifteen months in Guinea, with happy hearts Jessie and Herb headed back home to Tougan, leaving behind a missionary team which had been made stronger by their prayers, their hard work and their warm parental care. The lives of those young missionaries had been irrevocably changed. Cindy Westlake, former missionary to Guinea, said,

> Herb was driving my husband and me to another town. As we drove, I noticed he had tears running down his face. Finally, I couldn't hold back and asked him what was the matter. He said with heavy sobs, "These villages we're passing are without Christ. No one has ever told them of Jesus and His love." For the first time, I saw people as Herb saw them, and for the first time in my life, even though I was already a missionary, I felt a deep burden for the lost people of Guinea.

Thirteen years after Jessie left Guinea, she wrote a friend,

> We left a large part of our heart in Guinea, and our missionary vision was definitely enlarged during the fifteen months we served as director there. To this day, the Guinea field

and the missionaries who serve our Lord there are very high on our prayer list. We do indeed count it a privilege to hold the ropes for them. We can especially pray with understanding for the missionaries in Conakry, the capital city where we lived. We pray especially that God will give lasting fruit to His faithful servants there.

14

The Old Man (Le Vieux)

After their official retirement from Burkina Faso, Herb and Jessie had another job offer. Would they take care of the guest house and the Mission business affairs in Abidjan, Côte d'Ivoire for a two-year period? The Nehlsens jumped at the chance and happily returned to Africa after a brief break in the U.S.

They sent for the barrel and footlocker they had left in Burkina. Before they "retired," they had packed away some household things in what they called their "hope chest"—just in case they might return.

Missionaries passing through spoke in amazement of Jessie's ability to come up with something delicious to eat no matter how many people, expected or unexpected, showed up at any time of the day or night. Sometimes those who came were in desperate need of a listening ear and a sympathetic heart. One missionary wrote:

Our son had just been expelled from a school for missionary children and we were really hurting. We had never heard directly from the school about our son's infraction, and we had many unanswered questions. We felt great grief over the fact our son had to go through this experience, as well as the plane trip back to our country of service, all by himself without our support. And, of course, we were asking ourselves the big questions—how would this affect our son's faith and future, and would this mean the end of our missionary career?

"Coincidentally" I had a conference in Côte d'Ivoire a week later and arrived in Abidjan at Herb and Jessie's guest house. There I found understanding and comfort. They cared deeply about our family even though they had never met us before. They wept and prayed with me as I poured out my grief and anger. More than that, they affirmed me as a parent at a time when I was feeling like a failure.

Herb's advice to me was sound: "You need to go to the school and get your questions answered and tell them how much their handling of this problem has hurt you and your son." Later, at home, I told our son about my time with the Nehlsens and how they cared for us and had even wept over our pain. His teenage heart was touched when I told him that; he's never forgotten. I think having Herb there in Abidjan to minister to me, to be a caring pastor, was part of God's loving plan to get us through those dark days.

Jessie wrote home in her understated way,

We find our guests so appreciative of this home away from home. Herb is preaching every other Sunday in a church forty minutes away. For the next few months we will remain there at the church on Sunday afternoons for baptism classes, trusting that ten will be ready to be baptized before we leave. Please pray for revival within the established churches and that they will evangelize the growing number of Muslims in the country.

No one would have blamed this retired couple if they had used their Sundays to rest up and if they had simply concentrated on their assigned task at Mission headquarters. But that just wasn't Herb and Jessie's way. This country wasn't Burkina Faso; this city of over 2.5 million people wasn't Tougan, but nothing else was changed for the Nehlsens. They had the same priorities—to teach, preach and draw people to the Lord in every way they knew how.

And Wholesale Herb? Well, Abidjan was one fun place to be with its vibrant economy and its stores and markets full of bargains waiting to be found. Herb shopped till he dropped and established an unofficial store there at the Mission headquarters where he'd sell many of his finds to his missionary friends. "Canned peaches? I'll take a couple of cases of those. Missionaries will want to buy a can or two at that price. And what do you have in those boxes over there?" Jessie's "big, happy guy" was always on the shopping prowl.

Abidjan's international airport became Herb's home away from home. There were always missionaries coming and going, and part of his job was to meet

them upon arrival and then escort them back to the
airport when it was time for them to leave the country.
The trip from the guest house to the airport usually
took at least thirty minutes depending on the traffic.
Sometimes, though, that thirty-minute trip would
double or even triple in time if there was a barricade
put up by the military to check everyone's car documents or if an accident had slowed traffic to almost a
standstill.

One of the reasons for Herb's airport involvement
was that ICA (International Christian Academy) is located in Côte d'Ivoire, and many missionaries working
in West and Central Africa pass through Abidjan's airport every few months as they come to visit their children and then return to their places of ministry. The
children themselves come and go every three months
or so. A related aspect of all this airport traffic was the
endless string of problems related to luggage. Suitcases would be lost or would come in on a later flight
or would be damaged. It was up to Herb to make all
the extra trips out to the airport to straighten out these
problems. But he was the perfect man for this job. Not
only did he enjoy all the contact with missionaries, but
also, eventually, he got to know everyone of any importance at the airport. Airport employees called him
"Le Vieux" (the elder, a term of respect), and he'd talk
and laugh with them every time he did an airport run.

One visiting parent especially caught his eye. Marcia Braun was a missionary in Gabon. She frequently
came to visit her son, Josh, who was attending ICA.
Marcia's ministry back in Gabon was to manage the
Alliance bookstore, and in Abidjan she could find

more affordable French books and tapes than she could find elsewhere. So every time she came she'd entrust herself to some dubious-looking taxi and off she'd go scrounging through every Christian bookstore for "finds" to take back and sell in Gabon.

After Marcia's shopping forays, she'd come back to the guest house, often to a delicious meal prepared lovingly and without charge by Jessie. "They were protective of me and very generous," she remembers.

Marcia's determination and creativity caught Herb's eye. He saw that she was attached to a successful venture. Her little bookstore was turning over $100,000 a year, and his heart thrilled to think that that much Christian literature was being sold. Sometimes he'd drive Marcia where she needed to go, but always he would escort her to the airport for her return trip to Gabon. There, the hapless ticket agents and customs officials would meet their match.

"These are religious books," he would tell them. "They will teach the people in Gabon about Jesus, the only true way to God. By letting Madame Braun take these books back without paying duty you are helping Gabonese people find peace with God." Such would be the gist of each earnest speech delivered by a very persistent Herb in whichever language he deemed most appropriate for the occasion, Jula or French.

Marcia says, "He got hundreds of pounds of books through the airport without transport charges. I could then pass on this saving to the bookstore and colporteurs in Gabon."

One day, Steve was going through the airport and encountered the official in charge of customs. When he identified himself as Herb's son, the official volunteered that Herb was "a kind man; he always treated us with respect."

Previous generations of Christians frequently had what they termed "a life verse," a verse which had some special and lasting significance to them. Herb's was, "Trust in the LORD with all your heart and lean not on your own understanding; in all your ways acknowledge him, and he will make your paths straight" (Proverbs 3:5-6). For two years in Abidjan, Côte d'Ivoire, Herb and Jessie did the trusting and the acknowledging and didn't lean on their own understanding. And God did His part too—He made their paths straight, and those straight paths were a great help to nationals and missionaries alike.

15

The House of Mercy

The noon sun beat down on the baptismal tank there inside the walled enclosure housing the House of Mercy, a meeting place for "Muslim background believers" as they called them. Towering a head taller and half again as wide as the African pastor by his side, Herb stood knee deep in the shallow water as the first baptismal candidate started gingerly down the slippery steps toward him.

Jessie was in charge of the microphone held in front of the candidates as each of the eleven testified to his or her faith in Jesus' sacrifice. Not infrequently, fear caused them to forget what they intended to say. If a testimony lacked clarity, the microphone didn't move. Standing beside the candidate, Herb whispered a few words, and the candidate would expand the testimony. When Jessie was satisfied this person had given a clear witness for Christ, the microphone moved away.

Each candidate clearly understood the important and even dangerous step being taken that day. Fellow team member, Jim Patten, and the church leaders had been meeting with these candidates week after week, carefully studying the essentials of the faith which had taken root in each heart. They knew that for some of these candidates this public oath of allegiance was going to mean ostracism from family, employment hardships and even physical suffering.

Even though the new Christians were well grounded in their faith, they were still prey to both stage fright and even genuine fear as they stood in the water next to Herb that day. With a smile as big as his heart, he would repeat the familiar words, "Because of your testimony today, I baptize you in the name of the Father, the Son and the Holy Spirit." At that point, the African pastor took one arm, Herb took the other, and the two men lowered the candidate into the shallow water. And it was Herb's big hand that gently wiped the water off each face as eleven new creatures in Christ came up out of the water that day.

No baptismal service is ordinary, but this one was downright extraordinary! For one thing, this service was being held in a center, not a church, and some of the eleven individuals being baptized that day were former Muslims. Christian baptism is an exceedingly rare occurrence in a Muslim society because of Islam's strong hold on its followers. What made this event even more special was the significance of the day—it was Herb and Jessie's last Sunday before returning once again to the United States.

Would this one be their final retirement? No one knew for sure, but as Herb preached, he gave his "last words." The African pastor introducing him reminded the congregation that in Africa a person's final words have great significance. Therefore, the people should listen with great care to "notre papa, notre vieux" (our father, our respected elder). And so, in Jula Herb poured out his heart to the nearly sixty adults sitting on mats in front of him. The listeners barely moved. Every eye was riveted on this aging man with an earnest face and an open Bible. As he finished his words, Herb told the people that he and Jessie would be praying for them. Emotion choked his voice. Gulping back sobs, Herb turned and sat down on a mat beside the table he had just used as a pulpit. The people murmured and sighed. The big old man was crying.

Yes, Herb and Jessie had come back to Africa a third time since their retirement and were once again finishing another short term, this time in Bouaké, Côte d'Ivoire, alongside their son Steve and his family. Steve and Amy were giving leadership to a team working to establish a congregation of mostly former Muslims. This team called their ministry "Pillars of Hope." Herb and Jessie were thrilled to have the opportunity to work alongside their family in this innovative work. They understood that Muslim converts have lots of issues with which to deal. For one thing, they often weren't comfortable in ordinary Christian churches; they didn't always appreciate the loud music and joyful dancing, for example. Also, while they were still in the "seeking" stage, they needed some privacy to find answers to their questions, privacy to protect them from

family persecution. And then, once they were converted, they needed a roof over their heads if they were
put out of their homes, something that happened all
too frequently.

Pillars of Hope, thanks to the prayers and gifts of
partners in the States, was able to buy land, erect a
center—not a church—and give it a neutral name,
House of Mercy. There, behind sheltering walls, were
some guest rooms and a large meeting place. This
meeting place didn't have benches, just mats on the
floor. During services, everyone took off his shoes before coming in. The men sat at the front, and women
at the back, just like Muslims do in their mosques.

Herb and Jessie knew how very difficult this work
was. Steve and Amy had told them of the painfully
slow progress being made toward seeing a body of
believers worshiping there. Their prayers, their interest and the fact that when Steve and Amy went on
furlough the team would be very shorthanded
pushed the elder Nehlsens to volunteer their services
to work on this team.

They had arrived with no delusions; they knew life
would be hard. Deep in a mostly Muslim sector of
the city, they rented a house, a small house which
trapped the heat and where neighborhood noises
continued unabated nearly twenty-four hours a day.
This wasn't a retirement home carefully planned
with every convenience; it wasn't even a particularly
comfortable house since, in addition to the heat and
the noise, it boasted neither comfortable chairs nor
an interesting view. Jessie's outstanding culinary
gifts had for their arena a minuscule, dark and poorly

equipped kitchen with nonexistent airflow. It was in this small and quite uncomfortable house Jessie and Herb chose to live and start to work. A huge plus for them was being able to use the language they had used throughout their missionary career, Jula. Jessie started up literacy classes on her front porch to help illiterate adults and to establish friendships that could later provide vehicles for sharing her faith.

This tall, graceful woman was also quick to show her love by using medical skills honed by decades of practice. Some days she'd be off to the women's prison, and when missionary Nansie Ike needed someone to follow up a contact, it was white-haired Jessie who traveled down the dusty bush road to explain the gospel in her quiet but authoritative way. She was seventy-one then, and her presence in an African crowd was always marked by turning heads and stares of admiration. Above average in height, and always carefully dressed, this slim grandmother with her curly white hair moved with grace and a quiet friendliness quite different from the jocular charm of her husband. In a society which venerates age, Jessie was watched and respected.

And Herb? Ever practical, ever ready for a chat, ever the entrepreneur, ever looking for ways to help people, Herb's life never lacked drama. Tuesday nights, until nearly midnight, you could find him drinking Arabic tea with the neighborhood men, trying to persuade them to leave their folk Islamic faith with its fear and legalism and turn to Jesus with His promise of hope and freedom. And then, bright and early the next morning, he would be off to sit down with another group and open his well-worn Jula Bible. In addition, Herb was always looking for ways to help his converted Muslim friends earn their daily bread. He was well aware of the persecution and ostracism they faced when they left Islam. This translated into diminished earning power, so Herb used his considerable entrepreneurial acumen to help these new converts earn a living.

Like one Wednesday morning, not yet 8 o'clock. Many men of seventy-three would be finishing their coffee before heading to the golf course. But not Herb. No, he's already bent over a table in a very conspicuous spot, carefully setting out carved curios made by his converted Muslim friends. People who didn't know this tall, friendly man no doubt wondered why he was selling African curios and artifacts, but Herb's friends weren't surprised to see him there. They know that what he's doing is true to form—he's just making use of his considerable personal influence and business expertise. He's set the prices himself, trying to get "top dollar" for his African friends. They are now his brothers in Christ, and Herb would do anything to make sure they and their children eat every day and have a roof over their heads. Plus, no doubt about it, few things interest Wholesale Herb more than finding a good deal and making money—especially if it helps the needy!

So, that Wednesday morning, a missionary bought a Christmas gift from this persistent man, and as she turned to leave, he called, "That apple salesman will be in your neighborhood today." Several weeks earlier, he had introduced her to a new convert who was trying to earn his living by selling apples. Herb wanted her not only to buy the apples, but also to introduce this salesman to other women in her neighborhood. He was asking quite a thing! Apples were a fairly expensive luxury, and he was asking her and her neighborhood to buy apples? It seemed he'd risk having his missionary friends consider him presumptuous rather than lose an apple sale for his African friend. Le Vieux could be pretty aggressive if it meant helping a needy believer.

Getting a well dug and functioning at the House of Mercy was something Herb helped do with lots of expertise, strong opinions on how to do it and a caring heart for the African men doing his bidding in that dangerous and dirty job. His prayer was that the new well would not only help the new believers, but also that the water would be shared with watching Muslims living nearby. He knew from his Burkina experiences that sharing precious water could have a softening effect on a hard heart.

Besides digging that well, the Nehlsens kept on offering Living Water to anyone who would drink. One day a woman came to Jessie's door propelling her obviously disturbed daughter in her wake. The daughter, an adult, was dehydrated, delusional and unable to open her mouth. Both Jessie and Herb recognized the spiritual battle going on in this pitiful woman and did all they could to help. After praying with her, they readied the little guest room behind their house and then helped her settle in.

For the next few weeks, caring for this woman became the Nehlsens' special privilege. They would pray with her themselves, and they would also invite believers from the House of Mercy to come by, sit with her, sing about the blood of Christ and pray with her. Jessie tended to her physical needs, and as the demon began loosening its grip on her mouth, she would prepare nourishing meals for her. The result of all this prayer and care wasn't what the Nehlsens would have chosen. The woman was eventually freed enough to eat and talk normally. Spiritually she made some progress singing and even praying in the name of Jesus. But neither she nor her mother seemed to make a definite and lasting commitment to Jesus Christ.

Despite this disappointment and many others like it, Herb and Jessie persisted in that difficult assignment until November 1999, when their final departure was scheduled. On their last Sunday in Bouaké, the baptismal service at the House of Mercy provided a poignant reminder of the "why" of their thirty-seven years in Burkina Faso, the "why" of their year in Guinea, their two years in Abidjan and the "why" of these fifteen months in Bouaké. Jesus told His disciples to evangelize, teach and baptize in His name. Two of His disciples, Herb and Jessie Nehlsen, were found in complete obedience to that directive as they once more said good-bye to Africa.

16

Herb's Last Party

Seleptember 2, 2000. Herb had gone to heaven. That morning, he finished breakfast, prayed and read the Bible with Jessie, and then went off to get boxes of warmer clothes they had stored away. He and Jessie were planning to leave the following week for missionary tour. They would be needing some winter clothes. Jessie heard a gasp—and he was gone. The paramedics couldn't revive him; he had already crossed Jordan. He was seventy-four.

A week later, family and friends gathered to thank God for Herb's life. They came from far and near—local friends from there in North Carolina, furloughing and retired missionaries who had known the Nehlsens in Africa, all four Nehlsen children along with their spouses, and Jessie and Herb's five grandchildren.

For both the Debbie Peck family and the Steve Nehlsen family, flying from Italy and Côte d'Ivoire respectively had added great stress to an already difficult week. Each one was reeling from this unexpected loss, trying to cope with the realization of just what a big hole Herb's passing would leave in their lives. But it was a victorious face the family showed at the memorial service. Although they wept freely and often, they also smiled, laughed and enjoyed special moments of reunion with friends and relatives they hadn't seen for a while.

To no one's surprise, a poised Jessie was the first speaker. With Steve standing protectively at her side, she spoke of the "good man" who had shared her life for almost forty-nine years. Her description of a man who "loved God, loved everyone, always looked on the bright side and never ever carried a grudge" brought tears to the eyes of her listeners. But Jessie's own remained dry as she carried on as Herb would have expected.

Becky's description of her dad centered around the word "generous"—generous with love, with hugs, with help, with his possessions, with cheer and laughter, with friendship, with thanks and with praise for Jessie.

Debbie spoke next, putting a "big" label on her father—a big man with a big heart who served a big God. This bigness flowed over into his spirit. "I never saw my dad discouraged," said the daughter who had once painted a plaque for him which quoted his favorite saying, "Hallelujah anyway."

And Steve. Back when Herb had spent his weekends preaching in Burkina's villages, he had been accompanied by a young disciple, Steve. As the memorial service continued, that disciple, now a missionary himself, called himself an Elisha who had just lost his Elijah but who, like Elisha, was asking for a double portion of his father's blessing. As Steve spoke, listeners tried—but failed—to imagine what a double portion of Herb's blessing would actually look like.

Herb's beloved Judi was the last family member to share. "Daddy would be quick to give God glory for all He's done, and he'd always praise my mother. Together they have allowed me a heritage for which I can only praise God."

As the memorial service continued, tears often turned to laughter—an explanation for why missionary colleague Nancy Pierce later referred to the service as "Herb's last party." Many of the memories shared by different people provoked laughter on that not-so-solemn occasion.

"Wholesale Herb" stories abounded too, like the time famine had hit so hard in Burkina Faso back in the early '70s. Herb started raising money, and as David Kennedy said, "At headquarters, we had the Mission famine account and the Herb famine account! God had blessed Herb as a fund-raiser."

No party is complete without music. So, with Amy leading, Stan Burns on the tom-tom and all the Jula speakers in the crowd standing, swaying, clapping and smiling, for a moment the audience was back in Burkina as the joyous strains of "Yesu Nana" ("Jesus Came") filled the chapel. Amy's final "Hallelujah" (á la africaine) was the perfect ending to a perfect moment. Was Herb singing along with the crowd, loud, off-key, clapping and waving his arms? Of course, no one knows for sure, but one thing was certain that day—everyone's perceptions of heaven were really taking a beating. Our Christian perceptions—no tears, receiving crowns, worshiping God, angelic beings—somehow had to be rethought now that Herb had been added to the equation.

Take the "no tears" in heaven idea, for example. Herb's tender heart toward His Lord meant that very, very frequently in both conversation and preaching he would weep as he spoke. He cried for the lost and the needy, it's true, but just as frequently he wept as he spoke of His Savior. Surely the Creator God is making an exception to the ruling on tears so Herb can fully express his adoration?

And the angels? Christians think of them doing God's bidding as well as worshiping before the throne. But now Herb is there. Somehow it's inconceivable that the quintessential wheeler/dealer isn't harnessing this angelic power to move things along a bit more efficiently on earth. At Herb's last party, someone spoke of his being likely to do some lobbying up there to get more angels sent to Africa!

The worship idea too presents some new challenges now that Herb is there. The day he was laid to rest, both Nansie Ike and her mother, Doloris Burns Bandy, spoke of an affectionate Herb who used to pick up his friends and twirl them around in an exuberant hug. Nansie's wonderings saw Herb finally greeting his very best Friend and twirling Him around as he at last saw his beloved Jesus for the very first time.

Even the Christian's view of the crown waiting in heaven shifted ever so slightly with Herb being the one to receive it. His granddaughter, Andrea Peck, wrote to Jessie saying that when she heard about Herb's death, the picture that kept coming to her mind was of him standing in heaven "with all the angels, singing, with a crown on his head with so many jewels he could hardly stand up!" At the funeral, Debbie added, "He's already thrown that crown at the feet of Jesus."

And is Herb now sitting on a cloud playing a harp? No. None of his friends can imagine that. Instead, they think he's talking things over with his fellow-builder, Tom Burns, as they make plans for May—hot season—when surely there will be a church roof to put on.

And so, today, Herb is in that heaven we wonder about. Jessie's job of "applying the brakes to his enthusiastic nature" is finished. No longer will her Scottish reserve and common sense help to temper the exuberance and impetuosity of her "other half." Her other job is far from finished, however. Until she joins Herb, she will keep on praying for their children and grandchildren and also for the African family she and Herb loved and nurtured in three different countries over a span of nearly forty-five years.

For the Nehlsens' friends, the memories continue—memories "of larger-than-life people, who nonetheless had the usual human frailties and foibles that we all have." The descriptions that come to mind as we think of Herb and Jessie are myriad: energetic, caring, hospitable, generous, positive, devout, jovial, affectionate, independent, innovative. The list could go on and on. The bottom line is that they have been people who love God, enjoy life and love people. And these qualities have made them good missionaries, appreciated by their colleagues and friends, both Africans and missionaries.

A friend summed it up as she spoke of the love expressed to her by Jessie and Herb: "Those of us who saw Herb probably came as close as we ever will on this earth to actually seeing Jesus."

Larger than life. Herb and Jessie's influence lives on today in Africa, in the buildings they built, the training programs they established and the many, many people who were eternally changed because their paths once crossed with two people who were larger than life.

Our Friend, Herb

Dedicated to Herb Nehlsen
as a tribute to the faithful life he lived

Our friend, Herb, was great in stature,
as well as big in heart.
Compassionate and caring,
right from the very start.

We'll not forget his smile, great bear hugs,
encouraging words, and such.
For these were the loving gestures
by which our lives were touched.

Who can forget his exuberance—
his joyful heart of praise?
He'd say, "Praise the Lord! Isn't He good?"
He honored Him all of his days.

He followed God's call to a far-off land.
He had such a heart for the lost.
Giving his life for the Burkinabe,
he counted not the cost.

His heart and helping hands reached out
to those in dire need.
Oh, what a generous spirit he had!
What an example in word and deed!

Praying for Muslims and others
to accept the Savior he'd known.
They came to understand and share his faith
by the Christlike love he'd shown.

He was devoted to his family.
You couldn't find a truer friend.
We'll all miss him, oh, so very much,
but this is not the end.

Life is really just beginning.
He's as happy as can be!
Can't you hear him shouting, "Hallelujah,"
as the Savior's face he sees?

His voice is heard above the crowd
that's gathered 'round the throne.
He's praising Jesus more than ever—
the pilgrim has come home.

He's been decorated by the King
with crown for righteous living.
For his servant heart was faithful
to the mission he was given.

He's reached the highest goal—
the one we're all reaching for.
May we live as he showed us how to live
'til we meet on the other shore.

—Margot Kennedy

Appendix:

The History of The Christian and Missionary Alliance in West Africa

Milton and Nancy Pierce

Herbert and Jessie Nehlsen . . . were products of their time and fit into a certain historical framework. They went to West Africa in 1956 at a crucial fork in history, just as the colonial era of pioneering, with the missionary in charge, was changing and the church was developing its own identity and agenda. These events helped to shape their ministry style as they worked among their beloved San people in Burkina Faso.

For the nearly seventy years before Herb and Jessie's arrival, pioneer missionaries had gone before them trying to establish God's kingdom in that dusty land. In fact, it was in 1890 that seven young students, with no money and no training, left the Midwest of the United States and stopped over in New York to inform Dr. Simpson of their intention of reaching the "dark Sudan" with the gospel of Christ.

Simpson and his group of disciples were fascinated with these young people and gave them lodging and food, and later paid the expenses to send them on their way by boat to the coast of West Africa. Of those first seven missionaries, four were dead within the first months, succumbing to a deadly fever, and one died the following year. Losing five out of seven—not a very auspicious beginning for reaching the Sudan!

But this did not deter the people from praying and giving back in the United States. Rather, it incited them to more prayer and to sacrificial giving so that new recruits could be sent to replace those who had been called home to heaven.

The beachhead for reaching the interior of West Africa at that time was Freetown in the English colony of Sierra Leone. Freetown was a developed town with stores, homes and transportation, even a railway leading a few miles into the interior. But from there inland the early missionaries had to travel by foot, trusting local carriers to show them the path and help carry their loads. There were swift-flowing streams, and often these missionaries had to use dugouts to cross over or travel their length. Fire, local wars, sickness and death were the constant enemy of this original brave band of Christ's soldiers. And they are our spiritual heritage today as we enjoy the fruit of what they began at the turn of the century. The interior of Sierra Leone was known as the "white man's grave" because so many people had died there. These were in the years 1890 until about 1920.

Robert Roseberry (or "loosebelly" as the West Africans called him—they could never pronounce his real name) was one of those early pioneers. He arrived in Sierra Leone in 1909, a single man who later married Miss Edith Plattenburg, a single lady missionary already on the field. It was the Roseberrys' dream to reach the vast unreached territories of French West Africa. Until this time, no Protestants had gained entry into the French colonies. But "at the close of World War I in 1918, when the peace treaties were being signed, President Wilson remembered Protestant missions. It was then that the St. Germain Treaty came into effect, opening French territories to the preaching of the gospel."

Mrs. Roseberry recounts in her book, *Kansas Prairies to African Forests,* "In 1919 we were appointed to open the first Mission station in French West Africa at Baro, nearly 300 miles inland from the coast."

R.S. Roseberry was a great man of vision and prayer. He made the first survey trips into the interior of what is now Mali and Burkina Faso [hereafter may be called Burkina], and during those trips he and his companions spent days in prayer, bathing their trip with this important ingredient of missionary achievement. These early missionaries were obsessed with reaching "the valley of the Niger River" which took them from the headwaters of the Niger in Guinea on up through Burkina and Mali to Tombouctou. Life was so difficult and so full of obstacles that at one point the Mission was referred to as "The Forlorn Hope." A stalwart missionary pioneer from Tibet was sent by Simpson to help out these early West African efforts, and he too lost his life here.

Others joined Roseberry and his companions and were assigned to work in the "dark Sudan." The cry was "On to Tombouctou"—that mysterious city of the desert where the gospel had never reached, although some early explorers had succeeded in surveying the area. The Alliance survey team finally did reach Tombouctou in 1924, and the Michael Kurlaks were assigned to this outpost. There Mrs. Kurlak became very ill, died and was buried beneath that desert sand. Other cities of West Africa claimed the lives of still more missionaries.

In Sikasso, Mali, in 1931, the dread yellow fever epidemic started. Mrs. Joder died first, followed by Mrs. Anderson and a couple days later her husband. All of them are buried in the Sikasso cemetery. In Bobo Dioulasso, Mary Freligh, daughter of Paul Freligh, died and was buried in the central cemetery of the city, and later the body of Mrs. Hyndman was laid to rest nearby.

The Alliance mission work in Upper Volta (Burkina Faso), had its beginnings in and around the city of Bobo Dioulasso [hereafter may be called Bobo]. Bobo, known as Sya by its original inhabitants, the Bobo-Madara, is a city with a long history. It was favored by the French colonial powers because of its more moderate climate, good water supply and key inland location. The Abidjan-Niger railroad from the coast arrived in Bobo in January of 1934.

In 1923, Rev. Paul Freligh and his wife arrived in Bobo. Paul's sister, Marie, also joined them there for a time. Marie was known as "tall Mary" (Mariama Jan), and it was she who later became one of the principle translators of the first Bambara Bible in Mali, along with Mr. Reed from the Gospel Missionary Union. Not all of those early pioneers were physically strong.

In 1927, the Frelighs left for furlough and did not return. At this time, Marie went to Mali. While in

Bobo, she had teamed up with Dora Hue (later Dora Bowman), and the two single ladies did some amazing travel on foot to distant places, preaching in the villages along the way. It is recorded that they went on foot as far as San in the French Soudan (now Mali).

Rich Johanson was originally from a South African family that migrated to the States. He and his wife Leah were both adept in linguistics and worked hard on the Bobo language. The fruit of their labors in the language were destined to go to the bottom of the sea in a trunk in that torpedoed ship that put the Bells and the Shaws on a raft adrift in the ocean on their way home during the war [see *In Peril on the Sea: The Story of Ethel Bell and Her Children Robert and Mary*, Book #14 in The Jaffray Collection of Missionary Portraits].

Richard must have been an intrepid pioneer. He visited a large number of the Bobo villages within 100 kilometers or more of Bobo. He obviously had a solid missiology. He started churches in key villages in and around what has become a metropolitan area. Places near Bobo such as Dougona, Kwa and Dingasso all had chapels that he built. He saw the value of learning the local language well. Here is his appraisal of his first term. "Learning language difficult. No one knew the extent of the four dialects. Thousands of kilometers to survey on foot, by bike and later by car. Much sickness. Authorities suspicious. People unresponsive."

Of his second term (1932-36), he wrote:

> Intensive evangelism with weekly visits in various directions on same day and evening. Response to message in some villages. Some misunderstood the message, giving it political

implications—freedom, redemption, salvation
from their present oppression (forced labor
under the French). By 1934, six village chapels
completed. Urgent need for rural stations ap-
parent. Santidougou established on a shoe-
string. . . . Short-term Bible school and literacy
classes held often. Since we now had several
hundred followers, authorities' attitude
changed completely to one of cooperation.

Richard wrote of his third term (1937-42):

Intensified evangelism with teams to unreached
villages. Building activities permit believers to
come for instruction, working part-time each
day. Chapel built (Santidougou church) with
$100 gift from a Florida lawyer; residence built
(Santidougou house) with $485 gift from rela-
tives in South Africa. (Bricks, blocks, lumber—
hand-worked, 26,000 man-hours.) School at-
tempted for boys. Only seven could be per-
suaded to come. Seven-year-old boys cannot be
spared from farming. Outstations built in
Natema and Makuma, where we lived part-
time. Teams go out from Santidougou to witness
as far as bicycles could carry them in a day. We
had a Bible House at the nationwide exhibition
in Bobo (1938) and got gold medal (on paper)
for the pavilion and two others for fruit, grain
and poultry.

Excerpted and adapted from *The Triumphs, Trials, Tidbits, and Trivia of
History: Seventy-five Years of Alliance Ministry in Burkina Faso,* by Milton
and Nancy Pierce, pages 8-10, 17-22, May 1997, 100 copies.

Not long after Richard Johanson wrote those words, two other pioneers, "Pop" and Helen Martin had an experience which would not only change the direction of their lives but would also determine Herb and Jessie Nehlsen's future. Reverend W.S. Martin, a veteran missionary who had buried his first wife in Mali's northern desert, later married schoolteacher and songwriter Helen Sherwood. Pop and Helen were teaching at the Bible school in Ntorosso, Mali when a desperate plea came their way, "Can't someone go and tell the people of Tougan about the Jesus Road? The Tougan region is so vast and no one there knows about Jesus."

God used this conversation to send Pop and Helen to Sourou, Upper Volta. And it was on the ten-year foundation of the Martins' ministry in the Tougan area that the Nehlsens began their missionary careers.

A Chronology

1890   The first Alliance missionaries are sent to West Africa, landing at Freetown, Sierra Leone, an English colony, where they establish a beachhead. Their efforts to enter French-speaking territories are refused.

1918   The French colonies are finally opened to the Protestants. The Alliance established a station in Kankan, Guinea, and uses it as a base for reaching the rest of French West Africa.

1919   The first Alliance missionaries arrive in Bamako, Mali where the Gospel Missionary Union has established a base. A decision is made to divide up the country and assign different areas to different missions. (This sharing of areas was called "Mission Comity" and remained a fact of life in West Africa until the mid-'70s.)

1923   Entry by the Alliance into the region known as the French Sudan, which now includes Mali and Burkina Faso.

1942   The departure of most Alliance missionaries due to World War II and the anti-American Vichy French government which occupied West Africa.

1945   The return of Alliance missionaries to West Africa after the war.

1956   The Nehlsen family arrives in Sourou, Upper Volta (now Burkina Faso).

1957   The first Malian and Burkinabe pastors are ordained.

1958   The reorganization of the West Africa Alliance Mission with headquarters in Kankan, Guinea.

1959   The administrative office of the Mali-Upper Volta Mission is transferred to Bobo Dioulasso, Upper Volta (Burkina Faso).

1960   The national church of Mali-Upper Volta is organized in San, Mali.

1972   Revival comes to the Mission and churches of the Mali-Upper Volta field.

1973   The Mali and Upper Volta Church separate to form autonomous churches.

1992   Herb and Jessie Nehlsen officially retire after thirty-seven years of missionary service.

1993   The Nehlsens are assigned to Abidjan, Côte d'Ivoire for two years.

1998   The Nehlsens are assigned to Muslim ministries in Bouaké, Côte d'Ivoire for fifteen months.

2000   Herb goes to be with the Lord on September 2; Jessie continues her ministries of prayer and hospitality.

2001   On December 15, Jessie, accompanied by Becky and Steve, attends Herb's memorial service in Tougan, Burkina Faso.

Adapted from information provided by Milton and Nancy Pierce.